Business Law and the CPA Exam

Second Edition

to Accompany

West's Business Law
Seventh Edition

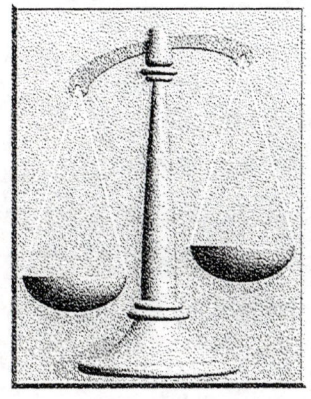

Prepared by

Steve Garlick, J.D.
Professor, Devry Institute of Technology

WEST
WEST EDUCATIONAL PUBLISHING COMPANY

An International Thomson Publishing Company

Publisher/Team Director: Jack Calhoun
Acquisitions Editor: Rob Dewey
Developmental Editor: Jan Lamar
Production Editor: Bill Stryker
Marketing Manager: Scott D. Person

Material from the Uniform CPA Examination Questions and Unofficial Answers, Copyright © 1980, 1981, 1982, 1983, 1984, 1985, 1986, 1987, 1988, 1989, 1990, 1991, 1992, 1993, 1994 and 1995 by the American Institute of Certified Public Accountants, Inc. is reprinted (or adapted) with permission.

Copyright © 1998
by West Educational Publishing Company
An International Thomson Publishing Company

All Rights Reserved
The text of this publication, or any part thereof, may not be reproduced or transmitted in any form or by any means, electronic or mechanical, including photocopying, recording, storage in an information retrieval system, or otherwise, without prior written permission from the publisher.

ISBN: 0-538-88002-3

2 3 4 5 6 7 C6 3 2 1 0 9 8

Printed in the United States of America

I(T)P®
International Thomson Publishing
West Educational Publishing is an ITP Company.
The ITP trademark is used under license.

Contents

Introduction v

Business Law and Professional Responsibilities
  Content Specifications vii

Common Law Contracts 1

Sales
  UCC Article 2 23

Negotiable Instruments (Commercial Paper)
  UCC Articles 3 & 4 47

Secured Transactions
  UCC Article 9 69

Suretyship 83

Bankruptcy 91

Agency 103

Regulation of Employment 117

General Partnerships (Partnerships) 125

Limited Partnerships 137

Corporations 143

Securities Regulation 155

Investment Securities 167

Documents of Title (Warehouse Receipts, Bills of Lading, and Others)
  UCC Article 7 171

Property (Real and Personal) 175

Insurance 193

Estates and Trusts 201

Account Liability 211

iii

INTRODUCTION

The Business Law section of the CPA Exam is a challenging, yet fair test of the candidate's knowledge of the law. There are many parts of the Business Law section that are equal to, if not more difficult than, portions of the Bar Exam.

Many candidates purposely forgo preparation for the Business Law section, in order to concentrate on other Accounting sections. Then, they later retake the Business Law section. With proper study and preparation, the candidate should attempt, and successfully pass, the whole exam on the first testing.

This supplement is an aid in that preparation. The supplement is not designed to teach the student/candidate the law. The text does this job very well. The supplement can provide needed direction for the serious Business Law student.

The author has reviewed CPA Exams for over 15 years, and has cataloged the most tested areas. The supplement is organized to conform to the text. This organization is for quick and easy student reference. An outline, provided by the AICPA, precedes the coverage of material included on the CPA exam. Take note of the percentages that the AICPA has provided.

For additional aid, the author has placed certain symbols for the student. A (T) indicates that the AICPA has tested on this legal issue. Either the AICPA has tested on this point of law or has assumed the students' knowledge within the body of the exam. The (TT) symbol indicates that the CPA Exam has tested on this legal point several times. Maybe the AICPA does not test on this issue during every exam, or every year, but the student should prepare themselves. Finally, a (TTT) indicates that the AICPA has tested on this legal principle a multiple of times. The student *must* be prepared for this question. Again, the text's CHAPTER, SECTION and PAGE numbers are listed after the questions for the student. Occasionally, a (W) has been placed before these symbols. The (W) indicates that this material is not covered in the West's Business Law text.

In addition, many CPA questions are integrated throughout for emphasis. The more candidates are exposed to the questions tested, the better they will perform. For this reason, nearly all of the sample Essay Questions and Long Objective Questions are also provided at the end of each Multiple Choice section.

The author wishes to make several acknowledgments.

The author would like to acknowledge the patience and good humor of Jan Lamar of West Publishing, and the assistance of Simon Maxwell, Beverly Owens, Martin Ward, and Fran Fletcher of Devry Institute-Kansas City, Missouri.

The author also appreciates the contributions from fellow Missouri Bar members Hank Koegel and Steve Schleicher. The author wishes to acknowledge the aid and suggestions of Mary Baker and Bret Curtis, accounting students at Devry-Kansas City. The supplement was written for just such dedicated people.

Finally, this author must acknowledge the aid and comfort of all my friends and colleagues during my illness. And in particular, I wish to thank my sister, Renie Garlick and Dr. Pat LaRocco for their kindness and help during my convalescence.

BUSINESS LAW & PROFESSIONAL RESPONSIBILITIES

CONTENT SPECIFICATION

I. Professional Responsibilities (15 percent)

    A. Code of Conduct and Other Responsibilities

        1. Code of Professional Conduct
        2. Proficiency, Independence, and Due Care
        3. Responsibilities in Consulting Services
        4. Responsibilities in Tax Practice

    B. The CPA and the Law

        1. Common Law Liability to Clients and Third Parties
        2. Federal Statutory Liability
        3. Working Papers, Privileged Communication, and Confidentiality

II. Business Organizations (20 percent)

    A. Agency

        1. Formation and Termination
        2. Principal's Liabilities
        3. Disclosed and Undisclosed Principals
        4   Agent's Authority and Liability

    B. Partnerships and Joint Ventures

        1. Formation and Existence
        2. Liabilities and Authority of Partners and Joint Owners
        3. Allocation of Profit or Loss
        4. Transfer of Interest
        5. Termination and Dissolution

C. Corporations

    1. Formation, Purposes, and Powers
    2. Stockholders, Directors, and Officers
    3. Financial Structure, Capital, and Distributions
    4. Merger, Consolidation, and Dissolution

D. Estates and Trusts

    1. Formation and Purposes
    2. Allocation Between Principal and Income
    3. Fiduciary Responsibilities
    4. Distributions and Termination

III. Contracts (10 percent)

  A. Formation
  B. Performance
  C. Third-Party Assignments
  D. Discharge, Breach, and Remedies

IV. Debtor-Creditor Relationships (10 percent)

  A. Rights and Duties—Debtors and Creditors

    1. Liabilities and Defenses
    2. Release of Parties
    3. Remedies of Parties

  B. Rights and Duties—Guarantors (Sureties)

    1. Liabilities and Defenses
    2. Release of Parties
    3. Remedies of Parties

  C. Bankruptcy

    1. Voluntary and Involuntary Bankruptcy
    2. Effects of Bankruptcy on Debtors and Creditors
    3. Reorganizations

V. Government Regulation of Business (15 percent)

   A. Regulation of Employment

      1. Payroll Taxes
      2. Employee Safety
      3. Employment Discrimination
      4. Wage Hour
      5. Pension and Other Fringe Benefits

   B. Federal Securities Acts

      1. Securities Registration
      2. Reporting Requirements
      3. Exempt Securities and Transactions

VI. Uniform Commercial Code (20 percent)

   A. Commercial Paper

      1. Types of Negotiable Instruments
      2. Requisites of Negotiability
      3. Transfer and Negotiation
      4. Holders and Holders in Due Course
      5. Liabilities, Defenses, and Rights
      6. Discharge

   B. Sales

      1. Contracts Covering Goods
      2. Warranties
      3. Product Liability
      4. Risk of Loss
      5. Performance and Obligations
      6. Remedies and Defenses

   C. Secured Transactions

      1. Attachment of Security Interests
      2. Perfection of Security Interests
      3. Priorities
      4. Rights of Debtors, Creditors, and Third Parties

VII. Property (10 percent)

   A. Real Property

   1. Types of Ownership
   2. Lessor—Lessee
   3. Deeds, Recording, Title Defects, and Title Insurance
   4. Mortgages and Other Liens
   5. Fixtures
   6. Environmental Liability

   B. Personal Property

   1. Types of Ownership
   2. Bailments

   C. Fire and Casualty Insurance

   1. Coinsurance
   2. Multiple Insurance Coverage
   3. Insurable Interest

COMMON LAW CONTRACTS

Common Law Contracts are 10 percent of the exam. However, since the types of questions are so numerous, the candidate should prepare for all possible questions.

I. Nature and Terminology

   A. Unilateral Versus Bilateral

   A UNILATERAL contract provides for an act in exchange for one promise (T), whereas a BILATERAL contract ("bi" meaning two) is an exchange of two promises. (T)

   B. The Objective Theory of Contracts

   The AICPA expects you to know that the courts impose a reasonable (objective) third-party analysis in contract interpretation. (T)

May 1983 #6

In determining whether a bilateral contract has been created, the courts look primarily at the

   a. fairness to the parties.
   b. objective intent of the parties.
   c. subjective intent of the parties.
   d. subjective intent of the offeror.

CHAPTER 12   SECTION 4   PAGE 206

   C. Licensing Statutes Versus Revenue Statutes

   LICENSING statutes are designed by the states to protect the public, while REVENUE statutes are designed to raise money. If one party creates a contract and is not licensed in that field (e.g. a paralegal as an attorney) then the that party cannot enforce the contract (e.g. a contract to make a will). However, if the statute was designed to only raise revenue, then the courts will allow that party to enforce the contract. (T)

D. Implied-in-fact Contract

An IMPLIED-IN-FACT contract is created by conduct, not by spoken or written words. Do not confuse an implied-in-law contract (a.k.a. Quasi Contract) with an implied-in-fact contract. A contract created by conduct is as legally binding as an expressed contract. (T)

November 1981 # 11

Where a client accepts the services of an accountant without an agreement concerning payment, there is

    a. **an implied-in-fact contract.**
    b. an implied-in-law contract.
    c. an express contract.
    d. no contract.

CHAPTER 12   SECTION 5   PAGE 207

II. Agreement

OFFER and ACCEPTANCE are heavily tested areas.

A. A contract offer must be definite and unequivocal. (T) A common law contract must contain the element of price. (T)

B. Advertisements (TT)

Newspaper ads or catalogs are <u>not</u> offers, they are only invitations.

May 1981 # 8

Harper is opening a small retailing business in Hometown, U.S.A. To announce her grand opening, Harper places an advertisement in the newspaper quoting sale prices on certain items in stock. Many local residents come in and make purchases. Harper's grand opening is such a huge success that she is unable to totally satisfy the demand of the customers. Which of the following correctly applies to the situation?

    a.   Harper has made an offer to the people reading the advertisement.
    b.   Harper has made a contract with the people reading the advertisement.
    c.   **Harper has made an invitation seeking offers.**
    d.   Any customer who demands the goods advertised and tenders the money is entitled to them.

CHAPTER 13   SECTION 1   PAGE 219

C.   Termination of an Offer

    1.   Death of offeror or offeree terminates the offer. In addition, no notice is required. (T)

    2.   Counteroffer by the offeree rejects the offer and creates a new offer. (The offeror and the offeree have exchanged places.) (TT)

    3.   Option contracts keep the offer open (irrevocable), but must be supported by consideration. (TT—see also consideration and UCC's Merchant's Firm Offer.)

November 1984 # 17

The president of Smith, Inc. wrote to Johnson offering to sell the Smith warehouse for $190,000. The offer was sent by Smith on May 1 and was received by Johnson on May 5. The offer stated that it would remain open until November 15. The offer

    a.   is a firm offer under the UCC since it is in writing.
    b.   is a firm offer under the UCC but will be irrevocable for only three months.
    c.   **may be revoked by Smith any time prior to Johnson's acceptance.**
    d.   constitutes an enforceable option.

CHAPTER 13   SECTION 2   PAGE 223

---

    4.   An offeror can revoke the offer any time before acceptance. (TT) However, the offeror cannot revoke his/her offer for a unilateral contract if the other party has commenced performance.

5. Rejection by the offeree terminates an offer. Remember, if the offeree categorically rejects, he/she cannot later accept, and a counteroffer is a type of a rejection. Offerors revoke and offerees reject. (T)

D. The Mailbox Rule (TTT)

A favorite topic on the CPA Exam.

1. General Rule—ACCEPTANCE at DISPATCH/MAILING (despite sender's error if sent timely) <u>and</u> REJECTION at RECEIPT. The main exception is if acceptance is sent followed by a change in the mind of the offeree for a rejection. Then, the first to arrive wins.

November 1982 #1

On October 1, 1982, Arthur mailed to Madison an offer to sell a tract of land located in Summerville for $13,000. Acceptance was to be not later that October 10. Madison posted his acceptance on the 6th of October. The acceptance arrived on October 7. On October 4, Arthur sold the tract in question to Larson and mailed to Madison notice of the sale. That letter arrived on the 6th of October, but <u>after</u> Madison dispatched his letter of acceptance. Which of the following is correct?

a. There was a valid acceptance of the Arthur offer on the day Madison posted his acceptance.
b. Arthur's offer was effectively revoked by the sale of the tract of land to Larson on the 4th of October.
c. Arthur could not revoke the offer to sell the land until after October 10.
d. Madison's acceptance was not valid since he was deemed to have notice of revocation prior to the acceptance.

CHAPTER 13   SECTION 3   PAGES 227-228

E. Conditions

The AICPA tests on "CONDITIONS," which could be a question concerning your knowledge of acceptance or performance.

1. A condition precedent tells the party when the duty begins and a condition subsequent tells the party when the duty ends. A third condition is called a concurrent. (T)The CPA Exam has tested this element in the area of Real Estate

Contracts. For example, earnest money must be returned to the buyer of real property if a condition in the contract (proper financing) is not fulfilled. (T)

III. Consideration

Very popular—it is almost guaranteed that one type of consideration question will be asked.

A. Definition

For contract consideration there must be a creation of legal benefit or detriment flowing to one of the parties in a bargained-for exchange. All contracts need consideration. (TT)

B. Adequacy

Courts do not weigh the level or adequacy of consideration. Therefore, a court will not rescue a party from a bad bargain. However, consideration must be present. (T)

C. Mutuality

If one party gets or gives up something, then the other party must also do one or the other. However, this is an old common law doctrine that is no longer taught in Business Law courses nor in law school. The AICPA has better areas to test the candidate in consideration, and has not asked this question very often. (T)

D. The Preexisting Duty Rule

The most obvious way to evaluate the candidates' consideration knowledge is to test them on the rule that any common law contract modification needs <u>new</u> consideration to be binding. (This is not so with a UCC contract.) (TT)

E. The Option Contract

In order to keep an offer open (option) the offeree must pay consideration to the offeror. (Again, this is not so with the UCC—see the Merchant's Firm Offer.) (TT)

F. Past Consideration

Past consideration is not good consideration, because there is no legal benefit/detriment flowing in a bargained-for exchange. (However, it will be a considered value for Article 3 of the UCC) (TTT)

6   Business Law and the CPA Exam

May 1982 #12

Bunker's son, Michael, was seeking an account executive position with Harrison, Inc., the largest brokerage firm in the United States. Michael was very independent and wished no interference by his father. The firm, after several weeks deliberation, decided to hire Michael. They made him an offer on April 12, 1982, and Michael readily accepted. Bunker feared that his son would not be hired. Unaware of the fact that his son had been hired, Bunker mailed a letter to Harrison on April 13 in which he promised to give the brokerage firm $50,000 in commission business if the firm would hire his son. The letter was duly received by Harrison and they wish to enforce it against Bunker. Which of the following is correct?

    a.   Harrison will prevail since the promise is contained in a signed writing.
    b.   **Past consideration is no consideration, hence there is no contract.**
    c.   Harrison will prevail based upon promissory estoppel.
    d.   The preexisting legal duty rule applies and makes the promise unenforceable.

CHAPTER 14   SECTION 3   PAGES 236-237

    G. Promissory Estoppel (a.k.a. Detrimental Reliance)

        Here, a promise can be enforced <u>without</u> consideration. If the offeror makes a promise that the offeror can reasonably expect that will induce an offeree to change his/her position to his/her detriment, then the courts will enforce the promise. However, this is not a contract. (T)

IV. Capacity

Not heavily tested, but the candidate should understand the difference between "VOID" and "VOIDABLE" in connection with capacity issues.

    A. Intoxication

        If the intoxication (alcohol or drugs) impairs the party's ability to comprehend the seriousness of what he/she is signing, then the transaction is voidable by the intoxicated party. The party may, also, disaffirm his/her contracts while he/she is intoxicated or for a reasonable time after sobriety. (TT)

    B. Minority

Common Law Contracts   7

A minor (the CPA exam will not expect you to know the state's age limit) can disaffirm his/her contracts while he/she is a minor and for a reasonable time after he/she reaches maturity. A minor cannot ratify his/her contracts while he/she is a minor. (T) This right belongs to the minor, and not to his/her parents. The minor may have to make restitution, especially in the area of necessities. (TT)

V. Genuineness of Assent

   A. Mistake of Fact

   The AICPA is more likely to test on UNILATERAL mistake (a mistake made by one party) and not BILATERAL mistake (both parties make a mistake). For instance, a contracting party cannot usually receive relief from a Unilateral Mistake. However, there is a testable exception. If the other party knew or should have known of the other party's mistake, then the courts do provide relief. (TTT) An example is a large math error. Also, there will be contractual relief from a mutual mistake of fact. The more proper legal analysis is that there is no contract at all, since there is no agreement. (T)

May 1983 # 14

Silvers entered into a contract which contains a substantial arithmetical error. Silvers asserts the mistake as a defense to his performance. Silvers will prevail

   a.   only if the mistake was a mutual mistake.
   b.   only if the error was not due to his negligence.
   c.   if the error was unilateral and the other party knew of it.
   d.   if the contract was written by the other party.

CHAPTER 16   SECTION 1   PAGES 261-262

   B. Fraudulent Misrepresentation (TTT)

   The candidate must know the elements of fraud! Not only will this knowledge be tested in Common Law Contracts, but it will be tested again in Accountant Liability and Security Regulations. Again, you must know the elements of fraud. The testable elements are:

      1.   Misrepresentation of a Material Fact
      2.   Knowledge of the Falsity (Scienter) by Defendant

3. Intent to Deceive by Defendant
4. Causation of Damages
5. Justifiable Reliance
6. Damages

Also, the candidate should know that, in contract, fraud is a voidable transaction. (T)

November 1981 #9

The element which makes fraud or deceit an intentional tort is

a. the materiality of the misrepresentation.
b. detrimental reliance.
c. actual reliance by the aggrieved party upon the misrepresentation.
d. scienter or knowledge of falsity.

CHAPTER 6   SECTION 2   PAGE 105
CHAPTER 16 SECTION 2   PAGES 264-265

C. Innocent Misrepresentation

This is also a voidable transaction. However, in this case, actual or constructive knowledge is not an element as it would be with fraud. (T) Also, there is no need to show gross negligence. A lack of reasonable care to discover the falsity is an element of NEGLIGENT MISREPRESENTATION. (T)

D. Duress

A physical threat to yourself or to your family would constitute contractual duress. Also, to threaten prosecution of a criminal offense is duress. Normally, economic duress (e.g. raise of rent or layoff) is not sufficient to warrant the contract as voidable. There is no "Reasonable Man" Duress Test.

E. Undue Influence

If one party uses undue influence over another (victim) party, then the victim of the undue influence can void the transaction. Undue influence can occur when one party has a fiduciary (trusting) relationship with another. (T) Examples of fiduciary relationships are: a parent to a child, a trustee to a beneficiary of a trust, or an accountant to a client.

VI. Legality

Very few questions in this area.

An illegal transaction is a void transaction. This means, unlike a voidable transaction, no one can enforce the contract. (T)

   A. Licensing

   If a party contracts in a area where he/she does not have a license and the license is regulatory, not revenue creation, then the transaction is void. (T)

   B. Covenants Not to Compete

   It is generally against public policy (illegal) to enforce a contract that would restrict a person's right to earn a living. Yet, courts will honor these covenants if the restrictions are reasonable. The CPA Exam could test in two circumstances: either the sale of a business or an employment contract. The covenant must be reasonable in terms of time and distance. (T) The CPA Exam also tests on this concept in the essay section.

VII. Statute of Frauds

This is a highly tested area. Not only will the AICPA expect the candidate to know the types of contracts that require a writing, but also the exceptions to this rule and the role of a memo.

   A. Land

   Any interest in land needs a writing for the contract to be legally enforceable. (TT) Exceptions include:

   1. Partial payment (T)
   2. Possession (T)
   3. Six-month oral lease (T)

   B. UCC

   See the UCC Sales (of Goods, not Services) section.

   C. One Year

   1. A contract, by its own terms, that will take longer than a year to perform must

be supported by a writing. The date begins from the date of the contract and <u>not</u> from the date of performance. (T)

2. Also, the key is not whether the contract performance is probable within the year, but possible. (T)

3. Full performance of the contract, within one year, takes the contract out of the Statute of Frauds. Therefore, the oral contract will stand. (T)

D. Surety/Guarantor

1. If one promises to a creditor to pay the debts of the debtor, then the promise of the guarantor (not the debtor) must be in writing. (T) A surety, however, is not protected by the Statute of Frauds.

2. Exceptions

The "Main Purpose Rule" is the one testable exception. If the "main purpose" of the guarantor is to benefit himself (for example, if General Motors were to guarantee the debt of a tire supplier), then the oral promise from the guarantor will stand. (T)

E. The Memo

It is a mistake to believe that the Statute of Frauds requires a complete written contract. The Statute can be satisfied with a memo. The memo must be in writing, signed by the party to be charged and contain the essential terms of the contract (legal description for land and quantity for the sale of goods). The memo may contain multiple pieces of paper. (T)

F. The Parol Evidence Rule

1. A highly tested area. (TTT) The rule simply states that there can be no outside evidence (oral or written) that will either add to, modify, or contradict contemporaneous discussions to an already integrated contract. Of course, the AICPA will test on the exceptions.

May 1983 #41

With respect to written contracts, the parol evidence rule applies

> a. exclusively to the purchase or sale of goods.
> b. to subsequent oral modifications.
> c. only to prior or contemporaneous oral modifications.
> **d. to modifications by prior written or oral agreements.**
>
> CHAPTER 17   SECTION 3   PAGES 290-291

2. Therefore, the rule does not prevent the introduction of evidence that explains the contract, such as an ambiguity (T), or discussions of terms discussed <u>after</u> contracting (fraud).

VIII. Third Party Rights

   A. Third Party Beneficiaries

   It is important for the candidate to keep clear the definitions in this area. There are INTENDED beneficiaries and INCIDENTAL beneficiaries. Intended beneficiaries can sue to enforce the original contract but incidental beneficiaries cannot. (T)

   1. Intended Beneficiaries

   Two types of intended beneficiaries include the CREDITOR beneficiary and the DONEE beneficiary.

   a. A creditor beneficiary relationship exists when a promisee makes a contract with the purpose that performance is not to go directly to the promisee but to a third party known as the creditor beneficiary. (T)

   1) This person is intended to benefit from this arrangement and can sue for performance. (T)

   b. A donee beneficiary relationship exists when one person gives performance not to the other party in the contract, but to another as a "donation" or gift (the donee). The prime example is in the area of insurance. An insured pays premiums to the insurance company for the clear intended benefit of the beneficiary. Once the insured dies, the donee beneficiary's right to payment vests. (T)

   B. Assignments and Delegations

12   Business Law and the CPA Exam

Remember, one ASSIGNS RIGHTS, but DELEGATES DUTIES.

1. Assignment

   a. In a creditor assignment the assignee must give the original debtor <u>notice</u> of the assignment. (TT)

May 1985 # 22

After substantial oral negotiations, Ida Frost wrote Jim Lane on May 1 offering to pay Lane $160,000 to build a warehouse. The writing contained the terms essential to form a binding contract. It also provided that the offer would remain open until June 1 and that acceptance must be received to be effective. On May 20, Lane mailed a signed acceptance. Lane completed the warehouse on July 15. On July 30, Lane assigned his right to receive payment to Reid Bank which did not notify Frost of the assignment. Two weeks later, Frost paid Lane $155,000 after deducting $5,000 in satisfaction of a dispute between them unrelated to the construction contract.

If Reid sues Frost on the contract, Reid will be entitled to recover

   a. the full $160,000.
   b. $160,000, less the $5,000 setoff.
   c. nothing, because notice of the assignment was not given to Frost.
   d. nothing, because it was not the primary beneficiary of the contract.

CHAPTER 18   SECTION 1   PAGES 297-298

---

   b. One cannot assign, nor can one delegate personal services and in particular if the assignment materially increases the other party's risk. (T) However, one can assign the right to receive money payments or the duty to pay a debt (e.g. a mortgage) (TT)

   c. Consideration is <u>not</u> required for a proper assignment. However, consideration does make the assignment irrevocable. (T)

   d. An assignee is subject to the same defenses as his/her assignor. (T)

2. Delegation

   a. The delegation cannot put a material burden on the delegatee (e.g. Personal

Services) (T)

      b. The delegator still remains liable unless there is a novation. (T)

IX. Performance and Discharge

    A. Performance

There are a few questions in this area.

      1. Substantial Performance

The law does not always require full or complete performance. In order for a party to sue and/or be discharged he/she must provide reasonable performance. SUBSTANTIAL PERFORMANCE is slightly less than reasonable but sufficient or reasonable under the law. The CPA Exam has also referred to it as "immaterial breach." With substantial performance the performing party may sue for his/her contract price, but less any damages for not providing full performance. (TT)

      2. Anticipatory Breach

A party need not wait for the other party's performance for discharge. If the repudiating party intends not to perform at the future contracted date, then the remaining party can claim ANTICIPATORY BREACH. In the UCC this is called instead "anticipatory repudiation"—see UCC 2-610. Still, the candidate should know the repudiatee's options for anticipatory breach. The repudiatee may: 1) sue immediately, 2) suspend his/her performance without threat of his/her own breach and sue later, or 3) continue to perform and wait for the repudiator to perform as contracted. (TT)

    B. Discharge

There are several ways by which a party may be discharged from the contract. The candidate should be familiar with them all. The testable examples include:

      1. Statue of Limitations

Here the statute runs from the date that the cause of action accrues (breach) (TT), and <u>not</u> from the date of contracting, as required by the Statute of Frauds.

      2. Accord and Satisfaction

If the parties are dealing with an undisputed definite (liquidated) amount, there can be <u>no</u> ACCORD and SATISFACTION. (TT)

3. Novation

With a NOVATION there is a release (discharge) of one party and a substitution of another party. (TTT)

November 1984 # 13

Mary is seeking to avoid liability on a contract with Jeff. Mary can avoid liability on the contract if

a. the entire contract has been assigned.
b. there has been a subsequent unexecuted accord between Jeff and herself.
c. **she has been discharged by a novation.**
d. a third party has agreed to perform her duty and has for a valuable consideration promised to hold Mary harmless on the obligation to Jeff.

CHAPTER 19   SECTION 3   PAGE 312

---

4. Impossibility

In order for a party to claim discharge because of IMPOSSIBILITY of performance, the event of impossibility cannot have been foreseen. (T)

5. Prevention of Performance

If Party A prevents Party B from performance, Party B is discharged. (T)

6. Illegality (T)

The correct legal analysis is that an intervening illegality discharges the party, since if the agreement was concerning an illegal act there is no contract for a discharge.

X. Remedies

A. Rescission

Contract RESCISSION puts the parties <u>back</u> in time as if the contract had not been made. (T)

B. Specific Performance

In order to receive SPECIFIC PERFORMANCE your remedy at law (money damages) must be inadequate. Therefore, the item must be unique. (TT) (e.g. land or rare personal property)

May 1983 #20

Myers entered into a contract to purchase a valuable rare coin from Eisen. Myers tendered payment which was refused by Eisen. Upon Eisen's breach, Myers brought suit to obtain the coin. The court will grant Myers

a. compensatory damages.
b. specific performance.
c. reformation.
d. restitution.

CHAPTER 20   SECTION 3   PAGE 328

C. Liquidated Damages

LIQUIDATED DAMAGES are damages contracted for prior to breach. Here the parties agree in advance what the damage will be for non-performance. Liquidated damages must be the best approximation, not a guess, and <u>cannot</u> be a penalty for non-performance. (T)

There are <u>no</u> penalties or punitive damages in contract.

ESSAY QUESTIONS

Since the AICPA tests extensively on Common Law Contracts, you should expect an essay question on almost any topic. The CPA has tested in the following areas:

MAY, 1982 NUMBER 4
CONTRACT MODIFICATION FOR LAND CONSTRUCTION

Issues Tested:

I. Contract Modification
II. Preexisting Duty Rule

ANSWER:

Under Common Law Contract rules, contract modification requires new consideration. This holding is because Common Law Contracts strictly apply the "Preexisting Duty Rule." Therefore if a professor signs a two year contract to teach Business Law and after the first year the college wishes to increase the contracted pay, the professor must provide new consideration for that extra pay. This is because the professor has a preexisting duty to work during the second year of his contract at the original contracted price.

However, there is an exception for the "Unforeseen Difficulty" (West's Business Law, 7th Edition, Chapter 14-Consideration, Section 3). For instance, if a building contractor contracted with an owner of land to excavate land for construction and an unexpected layer of bedrock was discovered, the contractor could demand extra money for the excavation of the bedrock. This is because if the contractor and the home owner knew about this layer of bedrock, then they would have agreed on a higher price.

Unfortunately, the AICPA has tested on this principle and would claim that the contractor can not be paid the extra money because of the Preexisting Duty Rule. This author believes the AICPA reads the Preexisting Duty Rule too strictly. In any event, the candidate should discuss both the Preexisting Duty Rule and the Unforeseen Difficulties problem and receive full credit.

The AICPA uses this example to test the student's knowledge that the UCC does not follow the rule that contract modification requires new consideration.

NOVEMBER, 1983 NUMBER 4
INTENTIONAL INTERFERENCE WITH CONTRACTUAL RELATIONSHIP

Issues Tested:

I. Breach of Contract
II. Statute of Frauds
III. Intentional Interference with Contractual Relationship

Bar Manufacturing and Cole Enterprises were arch rivals in the high technology industry and both were feverishly working on a new product which would give the first to develop that product a significant competitive advantage. Bar engaged Able Consultants on April, 1983 for one year, commencing immediately, at $7,500 a month to aid the company in the development of the new product. The contract was oral and was consummated by a handshake. Cole approached Abel and offered them a $10,000 bonus for signing, $10,000 a month for nine months, and a $40,000 bonus if Cole was the first to successfully market the new product. In this connection, Cole stated that the oral contract Abel made with Bar was unenforceable and that Abel could walk away from it without liability. In addition, Cole made certain misrepresentations regarding the dollar amount of its commitment to the project, the stage of its development, and the expertise of its research staff. Abel accepted the offer.

Four months later, Bar successfully introduced the new product. Cole immediately dismissed Abel and has paid nothing beyond the first four $10,000 payments plus the initial bonus. Three lawsuits ensued: Bar sued Cole, Bar sued Abel, and Abel sued Cole.

REQUIRED:

Answer the following, setting forth reasons for any conclusions stated:

1. Discuss the various theories on which each of the three lawsuits is based, the defenses which will be asserted, the measure of the possible recovery, and the probable outcome.

ANSWER:

Ironically, interference with contract is a tort. However, in order to sue for this tort there first must be a contract. The candidate must broach this point before the discussion of the tort.

For instance, A (Bar) contracts with B (Abel). However, C (Cole) interferes with this contract and commits the tort of intentional interference with contract relationship by offering B a better deal than A. First the student must tell the examiners the options that A has. A can sue B for breach of contract. The candidate should discuss why A has a legally binding contract with B. The candidate should also discuss possible contract remedies against B, and the potential defenses, if any, for B.

Next, the candidate should discuss the second option. The better second option is to sue C for the tort of intentional interference with contract. The reason why A should choose this option is punitive damages (remember the <u>Penzoil</u> case). There are no punitive damages in contract. Here, A could receive its actual compensatory (expectation) damages along with punitive damages.

After the option discussion, the candidate should discuss the elements of the tort of Intentional Interference with Contract. The elements include:

1. Valid contract
2. Defendant knew of the contract
3. Defendant intended to breach contract
4. Contract breached
5. Defendants interference is the proximate cause of the breach
6. Damages

Therefore, Cole is liable to Bar in tort for interference with contract. Bar could sue Abel for breach of contract, but since Bar can receive not only its compensatory but <u>punitive</u> damages from Cole, Bar's best option is to sue Cole. The contract is valid and meets the requirements of the Statute of Frauds. If Abel sues Cole for breach of contract, Cole could defend by stating that the parties contracted for the interference of another's (Bar's) contract. This is an illegal transaction, therefore the contract is void, and Abel cannot recover.

MAY, 1984 NUMBER 3
OPTION CONTRACT ON LAND

Issues Tested:

> I. Common Law Option Contract
> II. Silence as Fraud
> III. Statute of Frauds
> IV. Specific Performance

Jones signed an irrevocable 30-day option giving Lark the right to purchase a described tract of land owned by Jones at $20,000 per acre. Lark was director of King Corporation and knew that King had purchased through a nominee the adjacent land and needed Jones' land in order to build its national headquarters. Lark did not disclose this information to Jones and hoped to make a profit from the option. Jones had heard that Lark was in personal financial trouble and believed Lark would be unable to raise the money to exercise the option. Furthermore, Jones had no intent to be bound by the option at the time he signed it. The option stated that it was given in exchange for $100 and other good and valid consideration, but the $100 was not paid, nor was there in fact any other consideration.

Ten days later Jones learned that Lark had granted an option to King to purchase Jones' land at $30,000 per acre. Lark tendered to Jones full cash payment at $20,000 per acre within the 30-day period. Jones refused to honor the option. Lark brings an action for specific performance of the option.

Jones asserts the following defenses:

- Lark breached his fiduciary duty to King shareholders by personally entering into the options.
- Lark committed fraud by not disclosing all information regarding the proposed use of the land.
- The option given by Jones does not satisfy the Statute of Frauds.
- Jones never intended to be bound.
- There was no consideration given for his option.
- Specific performance is not a proper remedy.

REQUIRED: Answer the following, setting forth reasons for any conclusion stated.

1. Discuss the merit of each of Jones' assertions and then reach an overall conclusion based upon the facts presented.

ANSWER:

Whenever a student sees the AICPA test on a land contract the student must think: 1) Statute of Frauds, and 2) the differences between Common Law Contracts and the UCC.

Corporate directors and officers do owe the corporation fiduciary duties. A breach of these duties may result in punitive damages, compensatory damages, and/or a constructive trust.

Silence is not fraud unless the party owes the other party a duty to disclose. Lark does owe a duty of disclosure to the King Corporation, but not to Jones.

The option contract under the common law requires consideration to be binding. This option is not binding because the consideration was not paid. If the option contract is not valid, then Lark can offer and sell his land to the King Corporation. Specific performance would be the appropriate remedy if the land contract is valid. Therefore, Jones is correct. Since the transaction is for land, the UCC does not govern this contract.

NOVEMBER, 1984 NUMBER 3
DISAFFIRMANCE OF A MINOR'S CONTRACT

Issues Tested:

I. Voidable Minor's Contract
II. Ratification of Minor's Contract
III. Surety
IV. Covenant Not to Compete

A minor has the right to disaffirm his/her contracts while they are a minor and for a reasonable time after they reach majority. Also, a minor cannot ratify a contract while they are a minor. However, a minor can ratify a contract after they reach majority. This ratification can be by expressed words or by implication (conduct).

Covenants not to compete are enforceable, if the restrictions are reasonably related to time and distance.

If the surety is asked to pay the debtor's debt, the surety has several defenses. The surety may employ his/her own defenses or use the defenses of the debtor. However, the AICPA will test on the exceptions.

Bankruptcy and minority defenses are too personal in nature under the law. A surety cannot use these debtor defenses. Also while a creditor has a duty to disclose facts that impact the surety, the surety cannot claim his/her own defense of fraud if the creditor had no knowledge of the debtor's misrepresentations.

NOVEMBER, 1988 NUMBER 2
CONTRACT MODIFICATION

Issues Tested:

    I.   Oral Modification of a Common Law Contract

Contract modification may seem like an easy topic, but the candidate should separate contract modification under the common law and contract modification under the UCC. Oral contract modification contains several legal hurdles.

First, oral modification may violate the Parol Evidence Rule. Even if the modification passes this hurdle, the oral modification can bring the contract within the Statute of Frauds. For instance if the contract, as modified , would take longer than a year to perform or now involves the sale of goods at or beyond the $500 limit, then the contract requires a writing. Under the common law, unlike the UCC, contract modification must have consideration. A preexisting debt is not good consideration under the common law.

NOVEMBER, 1990 NUMBER 2
COMMERCIAL LAND DEAL

Issues Tested:

    I.   Statute of Frauds
    II.   Assignments
    III. Mailbox Rule

The candidate should know all the contracts that require a writing under the Statute of Frauds and the exceptions. The examiners have also tested on the issue of the memo. The Statute does not require a formal integrated writing. A party may satisfy the statute with a memo. The requirements of the memo include a writing, signed by the party to be charged, and containing the material terms discussed (land description, price quantity, etc.).

A party may assign to another the right to receive contract performance. The assignee doe not have to pay consideration for the assignment. However, the payment does make the assignment irrevocable. The CPA Exam tests on the types of transactions that are not assignable. The assignor cannot assign rights that are personal, illegal, denied by contract, or that would put a material burden on the initial obligor.

NOVEMBER, 1991 NUMBER 3
FRAUDULENT LAND DEAL

Issues Tested:

I. Fraud
II. Unilateral Mistake
III. Rescission
IV. Counteroffer Within the Statute of Frauds

The student should know that one of the grounds for the equitable remedy of rescission is fraud. The candidate should first examine the elements of the tort of fraud. These elements include:

1. A false representation of a material fact
2. Knowledge of the falsity (scienter)
3. Intent to deceive
4. Justifiable reliance
5. Damage

If the defendant can prove this *prima facie* case, the court will grant the equitable remedy of rescission (contract cancellation). However, a unilateral mistake is not grounds for rescission. If one party makes a mistake (unilateral) the court will not issue rescission. However, if the other knew of the mistake or should have known of the mistake, the court may grant rescission. The AICPA would rather test on this exception.

Under the Statue of Frauds, all interests in land must have a writing. The two main exceptions are the oral six-month lease and partial performance exception. Yet, even land offers and land counter offers must be in writing.

MAY, 1994 NUMBER 5
COMMERCIAL LEASE

Issues Tested:

I. Common law contract modification requires new consideration.
II. Offer and Acceptance and the use of an Option Contract.
III. Mailbox Rule
IV. Contract Discharge (destruction of the subject matter and impossibility)

NOVEMBER, 1994 NUMBER 2
BUSINESS TRANSACTIONS

Issues Tested:

       I.   Offer and Acceptance (Open Terms)
      II.   Mailbox Rule
      III.   Mirror Image Rule and Counter-Offers
      IV.   Assignments and Delegations
      V.   Creditor Beneficiary
      VI.   Statute of Frauds
      VII.   Remedies (No punitive damages in contract!)

NOVEMBER, 1995 NUMBER 4
SERVICES CONTRACT

Issues Tested:

      I.   Elements of a Valid Contract
      II.   Contract Breach
      III.   Contract Remedies

SALES
UCC ARTICLE 2

The UCC in general, and Article 2 (Sales) in particular, is a favorite topic for the CPA Exam. The questions covered in this exam can be as difficult as any seen on the Multistate Bar Exam. Regardless of the number of courses and the number of semester hours accounting students take in Business Law, law students have more exposure to the UCC. Therefore, the candidate should be forewarned as to the difficulty of this section.

Generally, the candidate should remember that Article 2 (which presently is in debate concerning changes) is slightly different than Common Law Contracts. Unfortunately, the AICPA will test on the differences in the UCC. However, there is some encouraging news. The AICPA tests in the major and less complicated areas (e.g. very few questions on title and risk of loss). Also, the UCC is a uniform law. It is not intended to be so complicated that practitioners could not function is this area. Keep in mind also that the UCC seems to relax the rules of the common law (e.g. no consideration for an option contract for a merchant) in order to keep commerce moving smoothly forward, not backward.

Finally, parties can contract out of the UCC. Therefore, the UCC only governs the transaction if the parties were silent on the point at issue.

I. Introduction to Sales Contracts and Their Formation

    A. Scope of Article 2

        1. Article 2 deals with the sale of GOODS only. In addition, the price of the goods has little application to the governance of Article 2. (T) However, do not confuse this with the UCC's Statute of Fraud section (2-601).

November 1993 #50

Which of the following statements would not apply to a written contract governed

> by the provisions of the UCC Sales Article?
>
> a. The contract may involve the sale of personal property.
> b. The obligations of a nonmerchant may be different from those of a merchant.
> c. The obligations of the parties must be performed in good faith.
> **d. The contract must involve the sale of goods for a price of $500 or more.**
>
> CHAPTER 21   SECTION 2   PAGES 342-344

      a. Also, one can be a nonmerchant and still be governed by the UCC. (TT)

      b. The UCC governs the sale of tangible and moveable goods. (T) The candidate should understand that the merchants are subject to special rules.

2. Good Faith

Every UCC contract is governed by the requirement of GOOD FAITH. (T) This element can not be disclaimed. (T)

3. Offer

    a. Gap Fillers (a.k.a. "Open Terms")

    The AICPA tests quite heavily on the concept of OPEN TERMS. These are terms that may be left out in the offer or in the acceptance, and still provide sufficient definiteness for a contract. (TTT) The candidate should know that price, delivery (time and place) and payment are open terms.

      1) However, quantity can never be an open term. (T) The reason is that while a judge can find a reasonable price etc., he/she cannot step in the shoes of the buyer and reach a reasonable quantity. Therefore, without quantity there can be no basis for a damages remedy. Without quantity there is no contract.

    b. Merchant

    Under the UCC, a merchant is a person who: (TT)

1) deals in goods of the kind involved in the transaction, or

2) holds him/herself out as a merchant, or

3) employs a merchant to act as his/her agent/broker etc.

The candidate should remember that the merchant is subject to certain limitations. These limitations, although not always tested, include:

1) Sales Contract of Modification (T)

2) Additional Term(s) in the Acceptance (the "Mirror Image Rule" does not apply to merchants.) (T)

3) The Statute of Frauds Confirmation 2-201(1)

4) Conditional Sales

5) Warranty of the Implied Warranty of Merchantability

c. Merchant's Firm Offer

This is covered nearly every year. The candidate should know the elements of the Merchant's Firm Offer. Unlike Common Law Contracts, a merchant must keep his/her offer open (option contract) even without receiving consideration. (TTT) Elements include:

1) Sale of Goods

2) Signed by a Merchant

3) Offer to remain open, without consideration, for a reasonable time not to exceed three months.

   a) Auction

   In a typical auction, the auctioneer is not making offers, but looking for offers. Here, if the auction is "without reserve," then the auctioneer can withdraw his/her petition for offers. (T)

November 1983 # 51

In order to have an irrevocable offer under the Uniform Commercial Code, the offer must

- a. be made by a merchant to a merchant.
- **b. be contained in a signed writing which gives assurance that the offer will be held open.**
- c. state the period of time for which it is irrevocable.
- d. not be contained in a form supplied by the offeror.

CHAPTER 21   SECTION 4   PAGE 347

---

4. Acceptance

   a. As stated above, under 2-207 merchants can add additional terms to the contract with the acceptance as part of the contract, unless the offeror expressly states otherwise. (TT)

November 1984 # 53

Bizzy Corp. wrote Wang ordering 100 Wang radios for $2500. Wang unequivocally accepted Bizzy's offer, but in doing so Wang added a clause providing for interest on any overdue invoices pertaining to the sale, a practice which is common in the industry. If Wang and Bizzy are both merchants, and there are no further communications between the parties relating to the terms, then

- a. Wang has made a counteroffer.
- b. a contract cannot be formed unless Bizzy expressly accepts the term added by Wang.
- c. a contract is formed incorporating only the terms of Bizzy's offer.
- **d. a contract is formed with Wang's additional term becoming a part of the agreement.**

CHAPTER 21   SECTION 4   PAGES 348-352

---

   b. In the above case, the modification would not be considered a rejection. (T)

Sales: UCC Article 2   27

      c.   Seller makes his/her acceptance by notice that he/she intends to ship conforming goods and then shipping them. (T)

      d.   When an offeror does not require a means of acceptance, 2-206(1)(a) states that acceptance can be made by any means of communication reasonable. (T)

5.   Consideration

Under 2-209 consideration is <u>not</u> required for contract modification. (TT)

6.   Statute of Frauds

One would expect this area to receive a great deal of attention by the AICPA. Although not heavily tested, this section is testable. Be forewarned that the Statute of Frauds section is in debate. Either an elimination or a raise on the dollar limit is expected.

      a.   Under 2-201 contracts of $500 <u>or more</u> require a writing. (T)

      b.   As is the custom on the CPA Exam, the exceptions to the rule also receive attention. Testable exceptions have included:

           1)   a specially manufactured item, and

           2)   an admission of the contract in the pleading. (TT)

May 1991 # 52

Gray Fabricating Co. and Pine Corp. agreed orally that Pine would custom manufacture a processor for Gray at a price of $80,000. After Pine completed the work at a cost of $60,000, Gray notified Pine that the processor was no longer needed. Pine is holding the processor and has requested payment from Gray. Pine has been unable to resell the processor for any price. Pine incurred storage fees of $1,000. If Gray refuses to pay Pine and Pine sues Gray, the most Pine will be entitled to recover is

    a. $60,000.   b. $61,000.
    c. $80,000   **d.**   **$81,000**

CHAPTER 21   SECTION 4   PAGES 355-357

28   Business Law and the CPA Exam

        c.   While contract modification does not require consideration, if the modification places the contract within the Statute of Frauds, then a writing will be required. (T)

II.   Title, Risk, and Insurable Interest

Business Law students do have some difficulty with TITLE and RISK OF LOSS. The AICPA tests in both areas. Accountants should be familiar with the terms of "F.O.B.," "destination," "shipping" and "carrier." This familiarity provides the candidate a better opportunity in this section.

    A.   Title

        1.   Identification of goods is a requirement for title. (T)

        2.   With a contract that states "Sale on Approval," title and risk of loss remain with the seller until the buyer accepts. (T)

        3.   With a contract that states "Sale or Return," title and risk of loss stay with the buyer until return. The buyer also bears the risk and expense of the return. (T)

        4.   Know the difference between a CARRIER (or SHIPMENT) case and a DESTINATION case. (T)

    B.   Risk of Loss

This topic is covered more extensively than Title.

        1.   Courts will look to the parties intent to determine how risk of loss is to be allocated. (TT) However don't forget, this investigation will be based on an objective (reasonable person) standard. And if nothing is stated in the contract, the UCC will allocate Risk of Loss.

        2.   The general rule is that the person who breached the contract will bear the risk of loss. (T)

        3.   Risk of loss passes at tender, if the seller is nonmerchant. (TT)

May 1984 #48

Nat purchased a typewriter from Rob. Rob is not in the business of selling typewriters.

> Rob tendered delivery of the typewriter after receiving payment in full from Nat. Nat informed Rob that he was unable to take possession of the typewriter at that time, but would return later that day. Before Nat returned, the typewriter was destroyed by a fire. The risk of loss
>
> **a.** **passed to Nat upon Rob's tender of delivery.**
> b. remained with Rob, since Nat had not yet received the typewriter.
> c. passed to Nat at the time the contract was formed and payment was made.
> d. remained with Rob, since title had not yet passed to Nat.
>
> CHAPTER 22   SECTION 3   PAGES 378-383

4. However, risk of loss passes on delivery, if the seller is a merchant. (T)

5. If the seller ships nonconforming goods, the seller still has the risk of loss. (T)

6. If the contract is F.O.B. loading dock, the risk of loss passes to the buyer with the delivery of the goods in the hands of the carrier. (TT)

III. Performance and Obligation

   A. A buyer may revoke his/her acceptance if the goods are nonconforming and if the nonconformity could not have been discovered within a reasonable time. (TT)

   B. A party's acceptance is definite, even if a new term has been added. (T)

   C. A party may be discharged from a contract for impossibility of performance, but the impossibility must not have been foreseeable. (T)

   D. Under the UCC a party can communicate his/her intention not to perform and the other party can claim "anticipatory repudiation." (TT) If a seller commits an anticipatory repudiation, the buyer can demand adequate assurance or cancel the contract. (T) Also, the buyer could wait for the seller to perform according to the contract. Remember, under Common Law Contracts this repudiation is called "anticipatory breach."

   E. The candidate should know the "Perfect Tender Rule" under 2-601. There is a violation of this rule if performance deviates in any respect from contract performance. (T)

F. Simply stated, if the seller sends nonconforming goods, he/she breaches the contract. (T)

G. A seller must hold conforming goods for the buyer and provide reasonable notice for the buyer to take delivery. (T)

IV. Remedies of the Buyer and the Seller

This a highly testable area! The candidate should very familiar with the options buyers and sellers have for breach of their contracts. Parties can demand multiple remedies as long as these remedies are not inconsistent nor a duplication. (T) It is also important to note what happens if either the buyer or the seller, as the party that breached, is insolvent. With insolvency comes more options for the nonbreaching party. Still, accounting students might consider "Balance Sheet" insolvency as the standard. However, the UCC, in the definition section of Article 1, states that an insolvent person under the UCC is the same as bankruptcy insolvency or if the party is not paying their debts as due. [(1-201(23)]

A. There are no penalties or punitive damages in an UCC contract! (TT) Contract remedies are designed to compensate parties or fulfill expectations. Under the UCC, like Common Law Contracts, remedies are not designed to punish individuals nor insure contract performance.

B. Remedies of the Seller

1. If the buyer wrongfully rejects, or refuses to accept conforming goods, the seller can resell the goods and receive damages, seek damages without resale, or cancel the contract. (TTT) The seller has cumulative remedies.

November 1989 # 52

Under the UCC Sales Article, if a buyer wrongfully rejects goods, the aggrieved seller may

	Resell the goods and sue for damages	Cancel the agreement
a.	**Yes**	**Yes**
b.	Yes	No
c.	No	Yes
d.	No	No

CHAPTER 24   SECTION 1   PAGES 402-405

2. If the buyer is insolvent (see above), the seller can reclaim the goods within 10 days (if the buyer misrepresents his/her insolvency, then there is no time limit) or stop delivery (this right ends when buyer receives the goods). (T)

3. Action for Price (2-709)

This section allows the seller specific performance! The candidate should know three instances where the seller can demand enforcement of the contract.

a. The buyer has accepted and title has passed

b. Conforming goods are either lost or damaged after risk of loss has passed to the buyer

c. The buyer breaches, the goods have been identified, and the seller cannot resell the goods for a reasonable price. (TTT)

November 1983 # 58

Marvin contracted to purchase goods from Ling. Subsequently, Marvin breached the contract and Ling is seeking to recover the contract price. Ling can recover the price if

    a. Ling does not seek to recover any damages in addition to the price.
    b. the goods have been destroyed and Ling's insurance coverage is inadequate, regardless of risk of loss.
    c. Ling has identified the goods to the contract and the circumstances indicate that a reasonable effort to resell the goods at a reasonable price would be to no avail.
    d. Marvin anticipatorily repudiated the contract and specific performance is not available.

CHAPTER 24   SECTION 1   PAGES 402-403

C. Remedies of the Buyer

1. "Perfect Tender Rule" violation by the seller.

For this violation the buyer has three options:

a. Accept all of the goods

b. Reject all of the goods

c. Accept some and reject the rest. (T)

2. The buyer needs identification for recovery of the goods. (T)

3. If identified goods are stolen, the buyer can ask for replevin. (TT)

4. If the seller repudiates the contract, the buyer can ask for cover (market price minus the contract price) plus his/her incidentals and consequential damages. Only a buyer may receive consequential damages. This is because the buyer normally plans to do something with the goods (resale as a wholesaler or retailer, or use them). However, the seller is only looking for the contract price, and the law will not anticipate his/her use with the contract money. (T)

D. Liquidated Damages. The UCC does allow either party to enforce a liquidated damage clause. The amount can not be any amount for lack of performance. The UCC provides for $500 or 20% of the purchase price, whichever is less. (T)

V. Sales Warranties

A favorite CPA section within the UCC. The candidate should not only be familiar with the warranties created by the UCC but also how these warranties can be disclaimed.

A. Warranties of Title (2-312) (TTT)

1. The seller warrants with the WARRANTY OF TITLE that:

a. he/she has good title.

b. he/she has no knowledge of liens. (T)

c. he/she has no knowledge of infringements.

2. Warranty of Title is also made by non merchants. (T)

3. Disclaimers

a. The Warranty of Title may be disclaimed, modified or excluded but specific language must be used. (T)

b. The disclaimer can be oral or in writing. (T)

B. Warranties of Quality

1. Express Warranties

A seller makes an express warranty by providing an assertion, affirmation, promise etc. about the quality of goods which become "part of the BASIS OF THE BARGAIN." (TTT)

May 1984 # 56

Which of the following factors will be most important in determining if an express warranty has been created?

a. Whether the promises made by the seller became part of the basis of the bargain.
b. Whether the seller intended to create a warranty.
c. Whether the statements made by the seller were in writing.
d. Whether the sale was made by a merchant in the regular course of business.

CHAPTER 25   SECTION 2   PAGES 416-418

---

a. This warranty may be made orally or in writing. (T)

b. This warranty can be made by non merchants.

c. A sample is an example of an express warranty. (T)

2. Implied Warranties

a. Implied Warranty of Merchantability (TTT)

November 1983 # 54

The Uniform Commercial Code implies a warranty of merchantability to protect

34 Business Law and the CPA Exam

> buyers of goods. To be subject to this warranty the goods need not be
>
> **a. fit for all of the purposes for which the buyer intends to use the goods.**
> b. adequately packaged and labeled.
> c. sold by a merchant
> d. in conformity with any promises or affirmations of fact made on the container or label.
>
> CHAPTER 25   SECTION 3   PAGES 419-420

        1) Made only by merchants. (T)

        2) The goods are fit for their ordinary or intended use.

        3) May be disclaimed either with the phrases "AS IS" or "WITH ALL FAULTS" (TTT) or by using conspicuous language that includes the word "MERCHANT."

    b. Implied Warranty of Fitness for a Particular Purpose

        1) Made by <u>all</u> sellers! (T)

        2) The goods are fit for their particular purpose. The buyer is relying on the seller's skill or special knowledge. Actual or constructive knowledge by the seller only is required. (T)

        3) May be disclaimed either with the phrases "AS IS" (T) or "WITH ALL FAULTS" or with conspicuous language. However, there is <u>no</u> requirement to include the words "PARTICULAR PURPOSE."

  3. Statute of Limitations (2-725)

In the UCC the plaintiff has 4 years <u>from the date the cause of action arose</u>. (TT)

VI. Product Liability

It is not clear why the AICPA should test in this area of tort law. What is even more confusing is why would the AICPA would test on such an unlikely area within the UCC section! It is not the purpose of this supplement to acquaint the candidate with the world of Torts and Product Liability. However, there are a few clear testable areas. The candidate should first remember that there are three types of torts: 1) intentional (focus on intent), 2) negligence (reasonableness), and 3) strict liability (dangerousness of the activity). Since very few manufacturers make products with the intent to harm their own customers, the candidate should concentrate on negligence and strict liability.

A. Negligence:

Here the defendant-manufacturer did not act as a reasonable person would have under similar circumstances. The elements of the tort of NEGLIGENCE include:

1. Duty

2. Breach of Duty

3. Causation

    a. Real cause or actual cause (the "but for" cause), and

    b. Legal cause or proximate cause (foreseeable)

4. Damages

B. Strict Liability

More plaintiffs would rather use Strict Liability, because there is no requirement to prove negligence (e.g. reasonableness). (T) The plaintiff need only show that a manufacturer put a defective product in the stream of commerce. The defect made the product abnormally dangerous. The elements of STRICT LIABILITY include:

1. A duty is owed by a commercial manufacturer or seller.

2. Breach of Duty (by placing a defective product in the stream of commerce). (T)

November 1993 # 54

To establish a cause of action based on strict liability in tort for personal injuries resulting from using a defective product, one of the elements the plaintiff must prove is that the seller (defendant)

a. failed to exercise due care.
b. was in privity of contract with the plaintiff.
c. defectively designed the product.
d. **was engaged in the business of selling the product.**

CHAPTER 8   SECTION 3   PAGES 132-135

3. Causation

   a. Real cause or actual cause (The "but for" cause), <u>and</u>

   b. Legal cause or proximate cause (foreseeable)

4. Damages

ESSAY QUESTIONS

As expected, the majority of the essay questions in Sales are those questions specific to the UCC. The candidate should know that the transaction in question is covered by the UCC. In other words, the contract involves the sale of tangible and moveable goods and not services or land. In addition, the UCC terms are mandatory only if a provision is absent in the contract. Contracting parties can contract out of the UCC.

Article 2A, leasing, is a new addition to the UCC. Applicants should prepare for potential leasing questions. A general rule is to answer the leasing question under Article 2 rules when the situation looks like an Article 2 sale. An example would be warranties under 2A. If the transaction has Article 9 characteristics, a secured transaction, then apply Article 9 rules.

NOVEMBER, 1981 NUMBER 5b
IMPLIED AND EXPRESS WARRANTIES

Issues Tested:

   I.   Express Warranty of Quality
   II. Implied Warranty of Merchantability
   III. Implied Warranty of Fitness For a Particular Purpose
   IV. Disclaimers

Maxwell was window shopping one day when she noticed an advertisement at Ultraclear Electronics for the sale of a shortwave radio for $495. Beneath the large caption indicating the sale and the price were the following:

- Never sold before below $550.
- Listen to the BBC, Radio Moscow, Radio Tokyo, and other international radio stations.
- Easy tuning, great reception, and made of the highest quality material.
- Don't hesitate, this is a limited offer on the buy of a lifetime.

Maxwell entered the store and proceeded to the place where the shortwave radio featured in the window was displayed with a similar, although smaller, sign extolling the virtues of the radio. Maxwell was examining the radio when Golden, an Ultraclear salesman, approached her. Maxwell told Golden that she was a great music lover and that she had long wished to listen to the Moscow symphony, the Moscow opera, and the music of the Bolshoi Ballet. Golden merely nodded his head and smiled knowingly. Golden said that at this price the company could not afford to give any implied warranties of quality beyond the replacement of the defective parts for ninety days.

When Maxwell got home and used the radio, she found it to be in proper working order, and that the shortwave reception was satisfactory for much of the world, but that it was not capable of picking up Moscow without severe static and at an exceptionally low audio level. Maxwell returned to Ultraclear and demanded that the radio be put in proper working order. The complaint department told her there was nothing that they could do about it, that the set was in proper working order and the fact that reception of Radio Moscow was poor was something she would just have to live with. Maxwell asserted that there had been a breach of warranty and demanded her money back. This was refused. Ultraclear's agent then informed Maxwell that she had no warranty protection. The company never "guaranteed" or "warranted" anything. In fact, the only thing stated with respect to warranties at all was Golden's remark clearly disclaiming any and all warranties.

REQUIRED:

Answer the following, setting forth reasons for any conclusions stated.

1. In the subsequent suit brought by Maxwell against Ultraclear to rescind the sale, who will prevail?

ANSWER:

The CPA Exam tests often on the warranties under Article 2. In this particular fact pattern, Ms. Maxwell should win.

First, Ultraclear has made express warranties with the captions from the window. The candidate should know that express warranties can be disclaimed, but only where reasonable and consistent.

Here the disclaimer is not adequate. Ultraclear cannot say the radio will pick up Moscow and then say that they are making no warranties. This is unreasonable and inconsistent. Ultraclear would argue that the radio did pick up Moscow, albeit not very well.

Next, there probably is no breach of the implied warranty of merchantability. There is probably nothing defective about the radio. Even Maxwell agrees. Ultraclear simply oversold the radio beyond "puffing."

Finally, Ultraclear has probably made an implied warranty of fitness for a particular purpose. Maxwell told Golden that she wanted the radio to listen to particular programs from Moscow. Golden nodded in approval. Ultraclear's best argument is that Golden properly orally disclaimed the warranty of fitness. However, this disclaimer is not in writing and not conspicuous.

MAY, 1982 NUMBER 5a
SALE OF GOODS (APPAREL)

Issues Tested:

    I.   Implied and Express Warranties
    II.   ature Disclaimers
    III.   Parol Evidence and Integration Clauses

Sure Rain Apparel, Inc., manufactures expensive, exclusive rain apparel. One model is very popular and sold widely throughout the United States. About six months after their initial sale to distributors, Sure started receiving complaints that there was noticeable fading of the color of the material. Many of the distributors sought to return the goods, recover damages, or both. Sure denied liability on the following bases: 1) there was an "Act of God," 2) there was no breach of warranty since the fading was to expected in any event, and 3) any and all warranty protection was disclaimed unless expressly stated in the contract.

The contract contained the following revisions relating to warranty protection:

    First: The manufacturer warrants that the material used to make the raincoats is 100% Egyptian long fiber cotton.

    Second: The manufacturer guarantees the waterproofing of the raincoat for one year if the directions as to dry cleaning are followed.

    Third: There are no other express warranties granted by the seller, except those indicated above. This writing is intended as a complete statement and integration of all express warranty protection.

Fourth: The manufacturer does not purport to give any implied warranty of merchantability in connection with this sale. The express warranties above enumerated are granted in lieu thereof.

Fifth: There are no warranties which extend beyond the description above.

The fourth and fifth revisions were conspicuous and initialed by the buyers.

Several buyers have commenced legal actions against Sure based upon implied warranties and express oral warranties made prior to the execution of the contract.

REQUIRED:

Answer the following, setting forth reasons for any conclusions stated.

1. Is Sure liable for breach of warranty?

ANSWER:

Sure will most likely prevail. The "Act of God" and the expectation of fading defenses are dubious. However, the disclaimers are adequate. In fact, Sure put an integration clause in the contract to prevent the inclusion of any outside evidence (parol) of further warranties.

MAY, 1982 NUMBER 5b
DELIVERY OF GOODS

Issues Tested:

I. Impossibility
II. Anticipatory Repudiation
III. Measure of Damages
IV. Specific Performance
V. Insolvency

Nielson Wholesalers, Inc. ordered 1,000 scissors at $2.50 a pair from Wilmot, Inc., on February 1, 1982. Delivery was to be made not later than March 10. Wilmot accepted the order in writing on February 4. The terms were 2/20, net/30, F.O.B. seller's loading platform in Baltimore. Due to unexpected additional orders and a miscalculation of the backlog of orders, Wilmot subsequently determined that it could not perform by March 10. On February 15, Wilmot notified Nielson that it would not be able to perform, and canceled the contract. Wilmot pleaded a reasonable mistake and impossibility of performance as its justification for canceling. At the time the notice of cancellation was received, identical scissors were available from other manufacturers at $2.70.

40   Business Law and the CPA Exam

Nielson chose not to purchase the 1,000 scissors elsewhere, but instead notified Wilmot that it rejected the purported cancellation and would await delivery as agreed. Wilmot did not deliver on March 10, by which time the price of the scissors had risen to $3.00 a pair. Nielson is seeking to recover damages from Wilmot for breach of contract.

REQUIRED:

Answer the following, setting forth reasons for any conclusions stated.

1. Will Nielson prevail and, if so, how much will it recover?

2. Would Nielson be entitled to specific performance under the circumstances?

3. Assuming that Wilmot discovers that Nielson was insolvent, will this excuse performance?

ANSWER:

Wilmot will lose on the argument of impossibility or commercial impracticability. Miscalculations and unexpected orders are not reasons for failure to perform. It is foreseeable that the supply and demand of products will rise and fall. Also, people make math mistakes every day. The UCC will not let a party out of a contract because they can't add! Implied in the facts is that Wilmot is not performing because the higher price of scissors.

Nielson can claim Anticipatory Repudiation. Therefore, Nielson can wait till March 10 for Wilmot to perform. That is an option available under the UCC. However, Nielson must mitigate his damages. Nielson can, under the UCC, seek the remedy of cover. The damages should be the difference between the contract price ($2.50) and the cover price ($2.70).

Nielson cannot seek specific performance. There is nothing within the fact pattern indicating that the scissors were unique.

Under 2-702(1) a seller (Wilmot) has the right to withhold delivery if the buyer (Nielson) becomes insolvent. Also under 2-705, the seller has the right to stop delivery in transit if the buyer is insolvent. However, there is nothing within the facts that excuses Wilmot from performance.

MAY, 1982 NUMBER 5b
RISK OF LOSS ON A SALES CONTRACT

Issues Tested:

I.   Risk of Loss

II. Breach of Contract and Risk of Loss

Dennison Corporation, a Los Angeles-based manufacturer, recently ordered some hardware from Elba Corporation, a Boston-based seller of fine tools. Unfortunately, all of the hardware was destroyed while in transit by the carrier. Further examination revealed that while one set of tools was shipped under terms F.O.B. Los Angeles, the other set was shipped under terms F.O.B. Boston.

REQUIRED:

Answer the following, setting forth reasons for any conclusions stated.

1. Which party will bear the risk of loss for each set of tools destroyed in transit assuming conforming goods were shipped?

2. Assume that Dennison also purchased some tools from San Francisco-based Drew Corporation which were shipped under terms F.O.B. San Francisco. The property was found defective upon arrival in Los Angeles. Which party will bear the risk of loss if the property is destroyed immediately after receipt?

ANSWER:

The parties may allocate risk by contract. If the parties do not allocate risk, then the UCC decides. The tools sent to Los Angeles were sent under a destination contract. Under a destination contract, risk of loss passes to the buyer Dennison at tender of delivery [2-509(1)(b)]. Therefore, since the goods were destroyed in transit, the seller Elba bears the risk.

However, the second shipment was sent under a shipment contract. Elba met their duty by placing the goods in the hands of the carrier in Boston. Therefore, the buyer Dennison must bear the loss [2-509(1)(b)].

Under 2-510, if the seller breaches the sales contract and the goods are destroyed immediately after receipt, the risk of loss should remain with the seller. The general rule is that the breacher should bear the risk of loss. If the defect is discovered immediately, then the risk of loss does not pass until the defect is cured or the buyer accepts despite the known defect. However, if the buyer discovers the defect after acceptance, the buyer can revoke his/her acceptance and the seller/breacher will bear the loss.

MAY, 1985 NUMBER 2
BUILDING CONTRACT AND MODIFICATION OF A SALES CONTRACT

Issues Tested:

I. Governance of the UCC
II. Statute of Frauds Within the UCC
III. Modification of a Sales Contract
IV. Merchants' Confirmations
V. Partial Performance Exception to the Statute of Frauds

In any question that involves the analysis of the UCC, the student should tell the examiner why the UCC governs the transaction. Article 2 of the UCC deals with the sale of goods. Service contracts and land deals are common law contract questions.

If the sale of goods is for $500 <u>or more</u>, then the contract must have a writing. In addition, if the contract as modified is for $500 or more, then the modification must meet the Statute of Frauds test. If both parties are merchants, then the modification at $500 will not need a writing if one party sends written confirmation of the contract and the other party fails to object within 10 days.

Unlike the common law, UCC contract modification does not require new consideration. However, will the new modified terms be part of the contract? Under the "Battle of the Forms," new additional terms do become part of the contract. They would not become part of the contract if the original offer or contract stated that the contract could not be modified. The modification would also not be part of the contract if the modification would materially change the contract.

The AICPA has an obsession with land contracts. In this particular essay question the AICPA tests the candidates' knowledge of the exceptions to the Statue of Frauds. Remember, land contracts are not UCC transactions, but they do require a writing. A writing is not required if the transaction passes the partial performance exception. If the buyer and seller orally agree to a land contract and the buyer has made a payment along with possession and improvements, the oral contract will be enforceable.

NOVEMBER, 1988 NUMBER 3
STRICT LIABILITY (TORT) IN PRODUCTS LIABILITY

Issues Tested:

I. Elements of Strict Liability in Products Liability
II. The Commercial Supplier's Duty Under the *Prima Facie* Case
III. Defenses to Strict (Product) Liability

If a manufacturer of product (good) places a defective product in the stream of commerce, and that defect makes that good abnormally dangerous, the commercial supplier of the good will be strictly liable for injuries.

Therefore, the injured party will not have to show negligence on the part of the merchant. The candidate should be familiar with the elements of the tort. The candidate should, also, be prepared to discuss limitations of liability. First, the manufacturer meets its duty to the plaintiff by inspection, warnings and anticipating foreseeable misuse of its product. In addition, the defendant-manufacturer has the defense of assumption of risk. Finally, a product liability lawsuit may be filed even if workers compensation covers the plaintiff/worker's injuries.

NOVEMBER, 1990 NUMBER 4
IMPLIED WARRANTIES AND ENTRUSTMENT

Issues Tested:

    I.   Implied Warranty of Merchantability
    II.   Implied Warranty of Fitness For a Particular Purpose
    III. Void/Voidable Title
    IV. Entrustment

The UCC differs from Common Law Contracts with the inclusion of implied warranties. The candidate should be able to distinguish between the implied warranty of merchantability, made only by merchants, and fitness for a particular purpose, which is made by all sellers. Merchantability warrants that the goods are fit for their ordinary/intended use, while the warranty of fitness holds that the goods are fit for the particular use of the buyer. The candidate should know how each warranty is disclaimed. "AS IS" will disclaim both warranties. In this essay question, disclaimer was not an issue. Finally, the AICPA also included the warranty of title.

In addition, the AICPA has tested on the Entrustment rule. Generally, a party can only transfer the title he/she has. If the seller has good title, then he/she can pass good title. If the seller stole the item, then the seller has void title and can pass nothing. However, if a merchant is in the business of selling goods of the kind of a particular transaction, then the merchant can pass on good title. For example, if an owner takes his/her watch to a watch repair shop and the merchant sells the repaired watch to an innocent third party, the third party can defeat the claims of the original owner. In other words, the merchant had voidable title and passed good title under the Entrustment Rule.

NOVEMBER, 1991 NUMBER 4
RISK OF LOSS AND BREACH OF CONTRACT WITH THE SALE OF GOODS

Issues Tested:

    I.   Risk of Loss
    II.   The Sending of Nonconforming Goods
    III. Perfect Tender Rule
    IV. Acceptance

The risk of loss rules can be complex, yet the AICPA tests on the more common rules. The candidate should tell the examiners that unless the parties have covered risk of loss in their contract, then the UCC applies. If the transaction is a carrier case (F.O.B. carrier, F.O.B. shipment, or F.O.B. seller's dock), risk of loss passes to buyer when the goods are delivered to the carrier. Risk remains with the seller if the seller sends nonconforming goods. The UCC would consider this shipment to be a breach, and consequently, the UCC's risk of loss rules do not apply. The candidate could, also, find relief for the buyer by stating that the seller rejected the original contract by sending nonconforming goods.

The UCC preserves the "Perfect Tender Rule." Therefore, if the seller's performance deviates in any respect, the buyer may reject all the goods, accept all the goods, or accept some and reject the rest. If the buyer rejects the goods, he/she should provide the seller with timely notice.

NOVEMBER, 1992 NUMBER 5
THE UNIQUENESS OF ARTICLE 2

Issues Tested:

      I.   Definition of Merchant
      II.   Merchant's Firm Offer
      III.   Statute of Frauds (Exception—Oral Contract Confirmation)
      IV.   Acceptance (UCC does not follow the "Mirror Image Rule")
      V.   "Battle of the Forms"

The candidate should expect the AICPA to test on the differences between Common Law Contracts and the UCC.

In this essay question, the AICPA tested on the Merchant's Firm Offer. The candidate should first discuss why the transaction is within the UCC (sale of goods). Next, discuss why the particular party is a merchant. Finally, discuss the elements of the Merchant's Firm Offer. Remember, the UCC relaxes rule of the common law option contract by not requiring consideration. However, the option must be signed by a merchant and be kept open for a reasonable time not to exceed three months.

Another difference is the UCC's treatment of the Statute of Frauds. Here, if the sale of goods is for $500 or more, then the contract must be writing or be in memo form. Also, the UCC will allow one of the contracting merchants of an oral transaction to send written confirmation of the oral arrangement. If the other party does not object within 10 days, that party cannot use the Statute of Frauds as a defense.

While the UCC generally preserves the "Mailbox Rule" of acceptance at dispatch, the UCC does not follow the "Mirror Image Rule." In the UCC, when the acceptance adds an additional term, that new term by the old offeree is part of the original contract. This situation is called "The Battle of the Forms." The offeror can opt out of these UCC rules by requiring acceptance to be sent in a certain manner and by a certain time. The offeror can also require that the offeree's acceptance exactly match the offeror's original terms.

NOVEMBER, 1993 NUMBER 4
COMMON LAW CONTRACTS AND UCC

Issues Tested:

    I.   Unilateral Mistake
    II.   Statute of Frauds
    III. Acceptance/"Mail Box Rule"
    IV. Assignments

The AICPA, despite the other essay questions, also tests on legal issues that are nearly similar between Common Law Contracts and the UCC.

Under Common Law Contracts and the UCC, a unilateral mistake will not discharge a party from performance. However, if the other party knew, or should have known of the mistake, the court will grant discharge or reformation.

While the UCC has its own additional Statute of Frauds section, the UCC contract must still be in writing if the contract will take longer than a year to perform. The one-year requirement begins from the date of contracting.

LONG OBJECTIVE QUESTIONS
MAY, 1995 NUMBER 3a
SHIPMENT OF GOODS

Issues Tested:

    I.   Shipment/Destination Contracts
    II.   Risk of Loss/Title
    III. Shipment of Non-Conforming Goods, Breach and Open Terms
    IV. Specific Performance in The UCC

NEGOTIABLE INSTRUMENTS (COMMERCIAL PAPER) UCC ARTICLES 3 & 4

Articles 3 and 4 of the UCC should be of primary concern to the CPA candidate. First, the AICPA tests heavily on this section. Also, this section is also highly technical for the layperson. In law school the law student receives a semester's worth of lecture in this area, while accounting students may receive, at best, several weeks. However, the AICPA tests in this area as thoroughly as the bar exam does for lawyers.

Secondly, the Articles 3 and 4 have undergone extensive changes in order to place the law in the modern electronic era. Thus, the title of Article 3 has changed from "Commercial Paper" to the more modern "Negotiable Instruments." Still, the basic tenants of the Articles have not changed, and although the AICPA could test on the changes at any time, the major testable topics remain relatively unchanged. The AICPA still calls this section "Commercial Paper."

I. Types of Negotiable Instruments

The candidate should be familiar with the different types of instruments. In fact, the AICPA might display the instruments in such a way as to confuse the candidate. For instance, an instrument that looks like a note may be a draft instead and vice versa.

    A. Drafts

        1. Drafts are three-party instruments. (TTT) The candidate should recognize that the drawer of the draft orders one party, known as the drawee, to pay a third party, known as the payee.

        2. Drafts can be paid at a definite time in the future. If a draft is negotiable, then the instrument is called a negotiable time draft. (TTT)

48   Business Law and the CPA Exam

May 1985 #33

The following instrument was received by Kerr:

```
Madison, Wisconsin                                April 5, 1985

Sixty days after date pay to the order of Donald Kerr, one hundred and
fifty dollars ($150). Value received and charge the trade account of Olympia
Sales Corp., N.Y.

To:                                               New City Bank
Olympia Sales Corp.
U.N. Plaza,                                       by  Carl Starr
New York, N.Y.                                        President
```

The instrument is a

a.   negotiable time draft.
b.   check.
c.   promissory note.
d.   trade acceptance.

CHAPTER 26   SECTION 3   PAGES 437-440

---

3. Drafts can be paid on demand (also known as "presentment"). A check can be called a demand draft. Banks are drawees of a check. (TTT)

4. A trade acceptance is a type of draft that is used in the sale of goods. Here the seller is both the drawer and the payee, while the buyer becomes the drawee by accepting the goods. (TTT)

5. A draft is an order to pay. (T)

B. Promissory Notes

1. Promissory notes are two-party instruments. The maker/promisor promises to pay the payee either on demand or at a time in the future. (TTT)

November 1982 # 35

> September 2, 1982
>
> I, Henry Hardy, do hereby acknowledge my debt to Walker Corporation arising out of my purchase of soybeans and promise to pay to Walker or to its order, SIX HUNDRED DOLLARS, thirty days after presentment of this instrument to me at my principal place of business.
>
> <u>Henry Hardy</u>
>
> Re: $600.00 — Soybean purchase

The above instrument is

    a.   nonnegotiable.
    b.   **a negotiable promissory note.**
    c.   a trade acceptance.
    d.   a negotiable bill of lading.

CHAPTER 26   SECTION 3   PAGES 437-440

---

2.   A bank CD is <u>not</u> a draft. The CD is a type of note. (TTT)

November 1982 # 39

An instrument complies with the requirements for negotiability contained in the Commercial Paper Article of the Uniform Commercial Code. The instrument contains language expressly acknowledging the receipt of $10,000 by the First Bank of Grand Rapids and an agreement to repay principal with interest at 15% one year from date. This instrument is

    a.   nonnegotiable because of the additional language.
    b.   **a negotiable certificate of deposit.**
    c.   a banker's draft.
    d.   a banker's acceptance.

CHAPTER 26   SECTION 3   PAGES 437-440

3. An installment note is also a type of a note. (T)

C. The following are not forms of negotiable instruments under Article 3:

1. Investment Securities

Investment securities are covered in Article 8. (T)

2. Warehouse Receipts

Warehouse receipts are covered in Article 7. (TT)

3. Money (currency)

Money is not a form of negotiable instrument under Article 3. The purpose of negotiable instruments is to act as a substitute for money. (T)

II. Negotiability

The candidate should know 3-104 thoroughly. In fact, the student should not only study what makes an instrument negotiable and not negotiable, but also the exceptions. The exceptions to the general rule are a favorite areas of testing. Remember, in order to tell if an instrument is negotiable, the holder of the note must look to the face of the instrument. Under 3-104 an instrument must meet the following requirements in order to be negotiable:

A. Be in WRITING (T)

1. The instrument is still negotiable even if it does not use the literal language of the UCC. (T)

B. Be SIGNED by the maker of a note or the drawer of a check. (T)

1. The signature does not have to be at the bottom right hand corner (subscription). (T)

C. Be an UNCONDITIONAL promise (note) or order (draft) to pay. This is favorite test area.

1. Negotiable

a. If the instrument refers how the transaction arose. (TT) The instrument would be nonnegotiable if the instrument was governed or conditioned on the transaction.

- b. If an instrument is secured by a mortgage, the instrument is still negotiable. (TT) Do not be fooled. In fact, the instrument will be more marketable because of the secured interest.

- c. An instrument is negotiable, even if the instrument indicates which account must be debited. Accountants should understand this direction. (TT) However, if the payment is subject to the existence of the fund, then, due to the conditional nature of the instrument, it is now nonnegotiable.

- d. If the instrument is subject to certain implied or constructive conditions the note could still be negotiable. These acceptable conditions include good faith. (TT)

- e. When the words and numbers conflict on a instrument, the instrument is still negotiable. Words control in such an ambiguity. (TT)

2. Nonnegotiable

- a. An instrument that allows the holder the option to purchase land is nonnegotiable. (T)

- b. Governed or conditioned by a transaction (see above).

- c. Subject to the existence of certain funds (see above).

- d. While the ambiguity between words and numbers do not render the instrument nonnegotiable, the ambiguity of words does make the instrument nonnegotiable. (T)

- e. Just because the maker of a note states that it his/her _intent_ that the instrument be negotiable, the instrument can still be nonnegotiable. (T)

D. Sum Certain in Money

1. Negotiable

- a. An instrument can be paid in foreign currency. (TT)

- b. If an instrument is payable with interest at the contract (lawful) or at the judgment or legal rate of interest, the instrument is still negotiable. (TT) However, the rate cannot fluctuate.

    c. Payable at a specific interest rate, still makes the instrument negotiable. (T) The Revised UCC states that an instrument is still negotiable, even if the note contains a variable interest rate.

    d. If the instrument states that reasonable court costs and attorney fees are to be paid on default, the instrument is still negotiable. (TT)

2. Nonnegotiable

    a. Payable in stock. (T)

    b. Payable in gold. (T)

E. Be PAYABLE ON DEMAND or at a DEFINITE TIME

1. Negotiable

    a. Instrument is to be paid at a specific time but subject to acceleration (TT)

    b. Instrument allows prepayment (TT)

    c. Extension by the holder (T)

2. Nonnegotiable

    a. Extension by the obligor (maker, drawee or acceptor) (T)

    b. To be paid at a certain time after an event that is certain to occur, but uncertain as to the exact time (e.g. death). (TT)

    c. Instrument is not payable at a definite time (TT)

F. Be PAYABLE TO ORDER or to BEARER

This section is infrequently tested. The candidate should study the magic words of negotiability in order to understand how order and bearer paper are negotiated (transferred). In addition, the Revised Article 3 allows a check to say "Pay to" instead of only "Pay to the order of."

1. Bearer Paper

   A good general rule is that bearer paper will contain the word "Bearer." (T)

2. Order Paper

   A good general rule is that order paper should be issued to a specific named person with the words "or to his order." (TT) Be aware that the Revised Article does not require a draft to be "payable to order", the instrument may say "Pay To".

III. Transfer and Negotiation

   A. General Rules

   1. If an instrument is nonnegotiable, then the laws of contract and assignment must apply for transfer. (TT)

   2. An agent or a representative can sign in place of his/her principal and still properly negotiate an instrument. (T) Be aware that the rules for agent signatures are numerous and fairly complex. In fact, the Revised Article 3 has changed the rules on agent signatures. However, the AICPA does not test extensively in this area.

   3. In order to negotiate order paper, there must be endorsement <u>and</u> delivery. (TTT)

   4. In order to negotiate bearer paper, there must be delivery. (TTT)

November 1984 #49

In order to negotiate bearer paper, one must

   a. deliver and endorse the paper.
   b. deliver the paper.
   c. endorse the paper.
   d. endorse and deliver the paper with consideration.

CHAPTER 26   SECTION 6   PAGES 448-449

---

   5. Negotiation can create a "Holder in Due Course," but an assignment cannot. (T)

54   Business Law and the CPA Exam

B. Endorsement

1. General Rules

a. Since endorsements appear on the <u>back</u> of an instrument, endorsements <u>cannot</u> change the negotiability of an instrument. (TTT) This concept is not directly tested on the exam, yet the AICPA will expect the applicants to understand the significance.

b. Since no one is liable on an instrument, unless his/her name appears on it, endorsements are used to create liability. Therefore, the transferees can demand the unqualified endorsement of their immediate transferors. (TT)

2. Types of Endorsement

a. Blank

1) Changes order paper to bearer paper. (TT)

November 1992 # 35

West Corp. received a check that was originally made payable to the order of one of its customers, Ted Burns. The following endorsement was written on the back of the check:

> Ted Burns, without recourse,
> for collection only

Which of the following describes the endorsement?

	Special	Restrictive
a.	Yes	Yes
b.	No	No
c.	**No**	**Yes**
d.	Yes	No

CHAPTER 26   SECTION 7   PAGES 450-452

b. Special

1) Changes bearer paper to order paper. (TT)

c. Qualified

1) "Without Recourse" is a qualified endorsement, but blank and special endorsements are examples of an unqualified endorsements. (TT)

2) A qualified endorsement negates contract liability and limits certain transfer warranties to knowledge warranties. (T)

d. Restrictive

A restrictive endorsement does not change the negotiability of the instrument. (T) This is because the endorsement is on the <u>back</u> (not the front) of the instrument. The Revised UCC still holds to this principle, but limits a later transferee's liability for not honoring the restriction. (This would make an excellent future question.)

IV. Holder in Due Course (HDC)

The HDC (Holder in Due Course) status is the very core of Article 3. The purpose of Article 3 is to determine if the holder of an instrument is an HDC. The candidate should be prepared to know how a holder becomes an HDC and the special status the law places on the HDC. In brief, the HDC is subject to fewer defenses than the mere holder. In addition, the HDC can pass on his/her status to other transferees under the "Shelter Principle."

Although the status of the HDC is not as strong in consumer transactions due to the FTC Doctrine, an HDC is still king in commercial transactions. The candidate should study the HDC thoroughly and be prepared to answer certain questions on the HDC.

A) Creation of the HDC

1. A HOLDER

Under 1-201(20) a holder is person in possession of a negotiable instrument (see 3-104 above) and has good title. (TT) In other words, the instrument contains all necessary signatures, and there are no forgeries. If the instrument contains a forgery, then no one can be a holder since the potential holder does not have good title. If no one can be a holder, then no one can be an HDC.

> May 1984 #42
>
> In order to be a holder of a bearer negotiable instrument, the transferee must
>
>   a. give value for the instrument.
> **b. have physical possession of the instrument.**
>   c. take the instrument before receipt of notice of a defense.
>   d. take in good faith.
>
> CHAPTER 27   SECTION 1   PAGE 459

    2.   of a NEGOTIABLE INSTRUMENT (again see 3-104 above) (T)

    3.   who takes the instrument for VALUE

Again, the AICPA will expect the candidate to know the Article 3 definition of value and the exceptions.

    a.   While future services is value under contract law (see bilateral contracts), it is <u>not</u> value under Article 3. (TT)

> May 1984 #43
>
> Which of the following will not constitute value in determining whether a person is a holder in due course?
>
> **a. The taking of a negotiable instrument for a future consideration.**
>   b. The taking of a negotiable instrument as security for a loan.
>   c. The giving of one's own negotiable instrument in connection with the purchase of another negotiable instrument.
>   d. The performance of services rendered the payee of a negotiable instrument who endorses it in payment for services.
>
> CHAPTER 27   SECTION 2   PAGES 459-460

    b.   However, while payment of an antecedent debt is not value (consideration) under contract law, this payment <u>is</u> considered value for Article 3. (TT)

c. One is only an HDC to the extent that value is given, not promised. Therefore, a holder can be a partial HDC. (TTT)

d. Although not tested, the candidate should be aware of the FIFO rule for value. This is exactly the type of a question on which the AICPA should test an accountant.

e. Circumstances that are not value. The AICPA likes to test in this area, since this is an exception to the general rule.

1) Judicial sale or legal process. (TT)
2) Estate sale or bulk sale.

4. in GOOD FAITH

This is not a testable area for several reasons. First, this is one of the few times where the law actually investigates only what the individual is subjectively thinking. The normal standard is the objective third party approach. This called the "white (pure) heart, but empty head" standard.

Next, this area would call for too much speculation on the part of the candidate, and could be confused with the NOTICE requirement. However, an applicant could gain extra points on the essay question is this area. The issue should at least be raised, if possible. Finally, the Revised UCC Article 3 has changed the definition of "good faith" to conform with the definition of "good faith" found in Articles 2, 2A, and 4A.

5. and WITHOUT NOTICE that the instrument is

a. OVERDUE, or

b. has been DISHONORED, (T) or

c. any DEFENSE or CLAIM to it on the part of any person.

Very few questions in this area.

B. Defenses

An HDC is subject to universal or real defenses, but the HDC is not subject to personal defenses. The candidate should not enter the CPA Exam without a complete understanding of these defenses under Article 3.

1. Real or Universal Defenses (HDC is subject to)

    a. Infancy, Incapacity, Duress and Illegality

    This is an extremely complex area of Article 3. The candidate should read the old UCC 3-305(2)(a) and (b). Here state law will determine whether the above defenses will be real or personal. The good news is that since the CPA Exam is multistate/national exam, there is no way that the AICPA will test the candidate on the candidate's own state law. If the applicant can remember that the above defenses depend on state law, then that is all the student will need to know. The following are the standards for several personal or real defenses under 3-305. In order for the defenses to be real or universal defenses, the state law standards must meet the UCC standards.

TYPES OF DEFENSES	STANDARD FOR REAL DEFENSE UNDER THE UCC (Must consult state law)
Infancy (Minority)	Voidable [3-305(2)(a)]
Duress	Nullity (Void) [3-305(2)(b)]
Capacity	Nullity (Void) [3-305(2)(b)]
Illegality	Nullity (Void) [3-305(2)(b)]

    As 3-305 states, infancy is real defense to the extent that it is a defense to a simple contract. In other words, the UCC places a voidable standard for infancy. If one were to check state law, one would probably find that infancy is a voidable defense. Therefore, under the UCC, infancy would be a real defense.

May 1982 #38

Cindy Lake is a holder in due course of a negotiable promissory note for $1,000. Which of the following defenses of the maker may be validly asserted against her?

a. A total failure of consideration on the part of the party to whom it was issued.
b. A wrongful filling in of the amount on the instrument by the party to whom it was issued.
c. Nonperformance of a condition precedent to its transfer by the party to whom it was issued.

> **d. Infancy of the maker to the extent that it is a defense to a simple contract.**
>
> CHAPTER 27   SECTION 4   PAGES 466-470

Next, 3-305 says that incapacity, duress and illegality are "nullity" or a void standard. Therefore, if the state law matches the UCC void standard, then that defense is a real defense in that forum state. If the state only places a voidable standard, then that defense does not match the UCC standard and can only be a personal defense. The one true problem exists with how a state handles duress. Most likely, extreme duress (e.g. a gun to one's head) would have to be a real defense.

The above chart should help the student understand the analysis under 3-305. (The law remains relatively unchanged under the Revised Article 3.)

    b.   Forgery (execution by one who is without authority to sign). (TTT)

    c.   Discharge in Bankruptcy (TT)

    d.   Fraud in the Execution (Fraud in the Factum)

Fraud in the Execution differs from Fraud in the Inducement. In Fraud in the Execution the signer of the instrument has been deceived to believe the instrument he/she signed is not a negotiable instrument. For instance, if someone asks for your autograph, but you in fact have just signed a promissory note, this is Fraud in the Execution. An HDC would be subject to this defense. (T)

    e.   Material Alteration

While an HDC is subject to the defenses of a material alteration in the cases of a raised amount, the HDC is still an HDC for the original amount of the instrument. (TT)

2.   Personal Defenses (HDC is <u>not</u> subject to)

    a.   Breach of contract (TT)

    b.   Non performance of a condition precedent (TT)

c. Lack of consideration (TT)

d. The wrongful filling of a blank payable amount by the issuer (T)

e. Stolen instrument (if properly endorsed) or other claims of ownership. (TT)

f. Fraud in the Inducement

Fraud in the Inducement differs from Fraud in the Execution in that the signer knows that he/she is signing an instrument. The fraud that the HDC is not subject to is the inducement to sign. For instance, the seller fraudulently induces a commercial buyer to sign a contract for aluminum siding, when in fact the siding is made out of cardboard. An HDC is not subject to this type of fraud and still can demand payment. The commercial buyer's recourse is to sue the salesman. (T)

g. Remember, the transfer of a negotiable instrument to an HDC cuts off all personal defenses against the HDC. (T)

3. The Shelter Principle

a. If a person in possession can trace his/her ownership back to an HDC, then the holder will have the rights of an HDC. (TTT) Remember that in contract law, a transferee can obtain the rights that his/her immediate transferor has. Therefore, a holder who could not be an HDC in his/her own right can obtain HDC status. A good example would be a transferee who receives the instrument as a gift. The transferee could not be an HDC in his/her own right (a gift is not value), but will have the same rights as an HDC.

November 1984 # 51

Sample has in his possession a negotiable instrument which was originally payable to the order of Block. It was transferred to Sample by a mere delivery by Cox, who took it from Block in good faith in satisfaction of an antecedent debt. The back of the instrument reads as follows, "Pay to the order of Cox in satisfaction of my prior purchase of a desk, signed Block." Which of the following is correct?

a. **Sample has the right to assert Cox's rights, including his standing as a holder in due course and also has the right to obtain Cox's signature.**

> b. Block's endorsement was a special endorsement, thus Cox's signature was not required in order to negotiate it.
> c. Sample is a holder in due course.
> d. Cox's taking the instrument for an antecedent debt prevents him from qualifying as a holder in due course.
>
> CHAPTER 27   SECTION 3   PAGES 464-465

        b.   However, a person who committed fraud against the maker/drawer or knew of a similar claim or defense, cannot improve his/her position by later reacquiring the instrument. (TT)

    4.   The FTC Doctrine

Since consumers vote, Congress has tried to alleviate the problems that consumers (sale of goods or services) encounter when an HDC demands payment and avoids the personal defenses. Therefore, in a consumer transaction no holder can be an HDC. The AICPA does not seem to test in this area, even though accountants practice in more commercial areas. This doctrine would seem to be a prime subject for testing.

V.   Liability

The candidate should understand the types of liability present. The AICPA will <u>not</u> test on the underlying obligation liability. For instance, if the accountant does work for the client and the client writes a check or a note for payment, Article 3 does not explore the liability based on the accountant's work. If the check bounces (dishonor), not only does the client have liability on the instrument (Article 3), but also on the underlying obligation. There is no discharge on the underlying obligation just because an check has been issued.

Therefore, the candidate should study the concepts of contract and warranty liability in the UCC. Also, the CPA Exam will require the candidate to reconstruct the order of payment. This order is important when a holder wishes to find parties liable on the instrument. It is important to note that the order might not be in the order listed. Do not be fooled. Reconstruct the order from the original payee to the last endorser.

    A.   Contract Liability

A workable general rule is that no one has contract liability on the instrument unless his/her signature appears.

62 Business Law and the CPA Exam

1. Primary Liability

   A party who has primary liability is required to pay the original tenor of the instrument.

   a. The maker of a promissory note is primarily liable.

   b. An accommodation <u>maker</u> is primarily liable on the note. (T)

   c. An acceptor of a draft (when a bank certifies a check) is primarily liable. (TT) <u>No one is primarily liable on a check at issue!</u> (TTT)

November 1981 # 41

Dunbar is the holder and payee of a check. He takes it to the Federal Bank upon which it was drawn and has it certified. Which of the following is correct?

a. Prior to certification of the check, Federal is only secondarily liable on the check.
b. Federal is obligated to certify the check so long as there are adequate funds in the account.
c. After certification of the check, Federal is primarily liable, and the drawer is discharged on the check.
d. If Federal refuses to certify the check, the check will be dishonored.

CHAPTER 28   SECTION 1   PAGES 475-476

---

2. Secondary Liability

   Here the party is not immediately liable on the instrument.

   a. How to hold a party secondarily liable:

      1) Proper and timely presentment for payment of acceptance.

         A domestic, uncertified check must be presented within seven days of the endorsement. (T) [3-503]

      2) Dishonor of the instrument

3) Timely notice of the dishonor

Notice by a party, who is not a bank, in three business days. (T)

    b. Who has secondary liability?

        1) Drawers (TTT)

        2) Endorsers (TTT)

Endorsers are only liable to subsequent endorsers. (T)

        3) Accommodation Endorsers

   3 Other Testable Rules

    a. The signature of the payee is a necessary signature for order paper. (TT)

    b. A bank, under Article 4, can charge parties in any order. (T)

B. Warranty Liability

The AICPA rarely, if ever, tests in this area due to the complexity. The revised Article has made changes, but there is no indication of any change in the test strategy.

VI. Discharge

This is not an area of heavy testing.

A. Discharge by Payment (T)

B. Discharge by Renunciation

This absolute surrender of rights to the instrument must be in writing. (T)

C. Certification

Certification by a bank discharges the drawer and any prior endorsers, if certification is asked by the holder. If the drawer requests certification, then the drawer remains secondarily liable. (T)

ESSAY QUESTIONS

The student should be made aware of the statutory complexity of Article 3 and 4 of the UCC. In addition, states have passed changes to these uniform statutes. Although the changes do not have a high impact on the questions asked, the candidate should be prepared for the changes.

MAY, 1987 NUMBER 2
FORGERIES

Issues Tested:

I. Forgeries
II. Defenses

Of all the questions to ask about Article 3, forgeries are the toughest questions. The candidate must know the rules of forgeries, the consequences and the many defenses.

Remember, no one is liable unless his/her name appears on the instrument. Therefore, unless the signature is authorized under the rules of agency, the forgery has generally no effect. In fact, under the "Disappearing Ink Rule" the signature of the forged party "disappears" and the signature of the forger appears. This rule places contract and warranty liability on the forger. Another important general rule is that the person who dealt with the forger should suffer the loss.

A forged endorsement does not pass good title, and the loss will fall on the person who takes the forged instrument. The major exceptions are the "Imposter Rule" and the "Fictitious Payee Rule." Under both rules the maker or the drawer will bear the loss.

Forged endorsements and signatures are real defenses. Real defenses will defeat the claims of the HDC. However, the HDC may be able to sue his/her immediate transferor for breach of contract and for the breach of warranties. The HDC can claim that his/her transferor does not have good title and that all signatures are not genuine.

MAY, 1990 NUMBER 5
THE TRANSFER OF AN INSTRUMENT

Issues Tested:

I. HDC Requirements
II. Negotiability
III. Shelter HDC
IV. Negotiation

The student must know how a holder becomes an HDC. Therefore, the student must know three definitions:

1. Holder
2. Negotiable Instrument
3. Holder in Due Course

Also if a holder can trace him/herself back to an HDC, then the holder will also have the rights of an HDC. This is called the "Shelter Principle."

Order paper requires endorsement and delivery for proper negotiation/transfer. Bearer paper requires delivery alone.

MAY, 1991 NUMBER 3
TRANSFER OF AN INSTRUMENT

Issues Tested:

I. Negotiability
II. HDC/Shelter HDC
III. Negotiation/Transfer
IV. Ambiguity

Again the candidate must know the requirements for negotiability. However, the AICPA will probably test on the exceptions. For instance, a note is still negotiable despite a reference to a particular transaction. The instrument would be nonnegotiable if the instrument is conditioned upon the transaction.

Holders in Due Course must give value to be HDCs. A preexisting debt is not good consideration for contractual purposes, but it is value for Article 3.

HDCs are not subject to personal defenses, but they are subject to real defenses. Breach of contract or lack of consideration are personal defenses. The HDC can assert his/her claim, despite the defenses, unless the HDC knew of the claim at the time he/she took the instrument. The Shelter HDC can assert the same rights as the HDC can.

Nonnegotiable instruments are transferred by a contract assignment. A negotiable instrument is transferred by negotiation. Endorsement and delivery transfers order paper. Delivery alone transfers bearer paper.

Under Article 3, if there exists an ambiguity over the number or the words, the words control.

NOVEMBER, 1995 NUMBER 5
CPA REVIEW OF NOTES

Issues Tested:

   I.   Holder in Due Course
   II. Primary Liability
   III. Liability with a Restrictive Indorsement
   IV. Priority of Security Interest Under Article 9

REVISED ARTICLES 3 & 4
(RUCC)

Since the AICPA stills calls this section of the CPA Exam "Commercial Paper" and not "Negotiable Instruments," there seems no immediate need to worry about the changes. However, when a majority of states adopt the revised articles, candidates should prepare for the changes. Even if the AICPA does test on the changes, the Exam would remain relatively the same. For future reference, this supplement will include potential areas of testing. These areas are:

1. The Revised Article 3 has expanded the definitions of negotiable instruments to include money orders.

2. The definition of banks has been expanded to include S&Ls and credit unions.

3. Revised Article 4-205 makes a depository bank a holder even if a necessary endorsement is missing. There is no need to provide missing endorsements.

4. Customers have 30 days, not 14 days, to inspect their statements.

5. A note/draft containing reference to payment from a particular fund or source does not destroy negotiability under the old "unconditional promise" rule. Therefore, RUCC 3-106(b)(11) reverses old UCC 3-105(2)(b).

6. "Fixed amount" replaces "sum certain" and variable interest does not destroy a "fixed amount."

7. Negotiability is not destroyed if the printed form of the check omits the word "order."

8. RUCC reverses the presumption about ambiguity from "order paper" to "bearer paper."

9. Banks can postdate checks even before the date written on the check.

10. RUCC changes the presumption that a check is overdue from 30 days to 90 days.

11. Under the old UCC a transferor must honor the restrictive endorsement. Under RUCC a person who pays or takes the instrument for value can ignore the condition without liability.

12. RUCC has changed the definition of "good faith." The new definition says that "good faith" is "honesty in fact and the observance of commercial standards of fair dealing." "Fair dealing" is the added phrase.

13. RUCC has clarified the status of the HDC, signature, and warranty liability.

SECURED TRANSACTIONS
UCC ARTICLE 9

Article 9 of the UCC involves a secured transaction in personal property. A secured transaction in real property is called a mortgage. The AICPA tests extensively on Article 9, yet the testable areas are fairly predictable. The candidate should be able to differentiate between attachment and perfection.

The good news about this section is that the AICPA will not test extensively in the complex areas of perfection. Depending on the classification of the collateral, the ways to perfect can be complex.

I. Attachment

ATTACHMENT answers the question of seizure. If the secured party properly "attaches" his/her security interest to the collateral, the secured party has the right to seize the personal property (collateral) from the debtor.

    A. Elements of Attachment (Seizure)

        The candidate should be completely familiar with the requirements or the elements of attachment. (TTT)

November 1981 # 49

Which of the following requirements is not necessary in order to have a security interest attach?

    a. The debtor must have rights in the collateral
    b. There must be a proper filing.
    c. Value must be given by the creditor.

69

> d. Either the creditor must take possession or the debtor must sign a security agreement which describes the collateral.
>
> CHAPTER 30   SECTION 2   PAGES 521-523

1. The secured interest must be in WRITING. This requirement is similar to the state's Statute of Frauds in contract law. The writing should include a description of the collateral (to put other secured parties on constructive notice of the attachment), and the debtor (the party to be charged) must sign. However, a writing is not required if the secured party has taken POSSESSION. (TT)

2. The secured party must give VALUE. (TT) The usual manner for giving value is the creditor's extension of credit.

3. The debtor must have RIGHTS in the collateral. (TT)

II. Perfection (Priority)

The candidate should be familiar with the different ways to perfect.

A. Attachment

A secured party can perfect by attachment alone with a PMSI (Purchase Money Security Interest) in consumer goods. (TTT) A PMSI can exist in two forms. (The AICPA does not seem to test on these two forms directly, but the candidate should recognize the scenarios.) First, money is lent by the seller to the debtor for the purchase of the seller's goods (e.g. a furniture store lends you money specifically to purchase the furniture). The second situation is when a third party (e.g. bank) lends to the consumer specifically to purchase the furniture. This not for a credit card purchase. A PMSI may attach to non-consumer goods. However, a secured party is perfected by attachment alone, with a PMSI in consumer goods.

> May 1984 # 57
>
> Rich Electronics sells various brand name television and stereo sets at discount prices. Rich maintains a large inventory which it obtains from various manufacturers on credit. These manufacturer-creditors have all filed and taken security interests in the goods and proceeds therefrom which they have sold to Rich on credit. Rich in turn sells to hundreds of ultimate consumers; some pay cash but most buy on credit.

Rich takes a security interest but does not file a financing statement for credit sales. Which of the following is correct?

    a. **Since Rich takes a purchase money security interest in the consumer goods sold, its security interest is perfected upon attachment.**
    b. The appliance manufacturers can enforce their security interests against the goods in the hands of the purchasers who paid cash for them.
    c. A subsequent sale by one of Rich's customers to a bona fide purchaser will be subject to Rich's security interest.
    d. The goods in Rich's hands are consumer goods.

CHAPTER 30   SECTIONS 3 & 4   PAGES 523-528

    B.   Perfection by Possession

        1.   Common Law Pledge (e.g. jewelry) (T)

        2.   Negotiable Instruments (T)

        Possession is the method of perfection for negotiable instruments.

    C.   Perfection by Filing (a Financing Statement)

    FILING is the preferred method of perfection, unless the secured party is allowed to perfect by possession or can automatically perfect by attachment alone (PMSI).

        1.   Contents of a Filing Statement (TT)

            a.   A writing with the signature of the debtor.

            b.   Addresses of the creditor and the debtor.

            c.   Description of the collateral.

        2.   Accounts Receivables (TT)

III.   Expanding the Scope of the Security of the Interest or the Floating Lien Concept

    The security agreement may apply to other types and forms of property.

A. Proceeds

A debtor cannot defeat the security interest of the creditor by merely changing or exchanging the collateral. (TTT) For instance, the bank has a security interest in the debtor's commercial inventory. As the inventory is sold, the bank still has a security interest in the proceeds (the payments by the consumers).

May 1983 # 52

Gilbert borrowed $10,000 from Merchant National Bank and signed a negotiable promissory note which contained an acceleration clause. In addition, securities valued at $11,000 at the time of the loan were pledged as collateral. Gilbert has defaulted on the loan repayments. At the time of default, $9,250, plus interest of $450, was due, and the securities had a value of $8,000. Merchant

- a. must first proceed against the collateral before proceeding against Gilbert personally on the note.
- b. cannot invoke the acceleration clause in the note until ten days after the notice of default is given to Gilbert.
- c. must give Gilbert 30 days after default in which to refinance the loan.
- **d. is entitled to proceed against Gilbert on either the note or the collateral or both.**

CHAPTER 30   SECTION 5   PAGES 530-532

B. After-Acquired Property

The security agreement can cover not only the specific collateral in the agreement, but the loan can attach to other types of property acquired by the debtor.

C. Future Advances

The debtor may have a line of credit that allows the creditor to attach his/her security interest to specific personal property as collateral, and any future loans will use the same personal property as collateral.

IV. Priority Rules

This is the crux of Article 9. Who will be the first vulture (creditor) to pick at the carcass (the collateral)? The priority rules of Article 9 will answer this question. The priority rules are, in reality, extremely complex. The candidate should keep in mind a few general rules (for objective and essay questions) and a few specific exceptions.

A. General Rules

If the applicant is having difficulty with the priority rules, remember these general principles:

1. If two competing creditors have only attached, the first to attach wins.

2. If two competing creditors have attached and perfected, generally the first to perfect (e.g. possession) wins. (TTT)

3. If one creditor has only attached and the other creditor has perfected, the creditor who has perfected will generally win. (TT)

May 1989 # 60

Burn Manufacturing borrowed $500,000 from Howard Finance Co., secured by Burn's present and future inventory, accounts receivable, and the proceeds thereof. The parties signed a financing statement that described the collateral and it was filed in the appropriate state office. Burn subsequently defaulted in the repayment of the loan and Howard attempted to enforce its security interest. Burn contended that Howard's security interest was unenforceable. In addition, Green, who subsequently gave credit to Burn without knowledge of Howard's alleged security interest, is also attempting to defeat Howard's alleged security interest. The security interest in question is valid with respect to

a. both Burn and Green.
b. neither Burn nor Green.
c. Burn but not Green.
d. Green but not Burn.

CHAPTER 30   SECTION 6   PAGES 532-536

B. Specific Situations

The AICPA does test on a few specific fact patterns.

1. A filing provides priority. A PMSI in equipment that is filed within 10 days of

attachment provides top priority and even beats a bankruptcy trustee or other secured parties. (TT)

November 1984 # 58

Milo Manufacturing Corp. sells baseball equipment to distributors, who in turn sell the equipment to various retailers throughout the U.S. The retailers then sell the equipment to consumers who use the equipment for their own personal use. In all cases, the equipment is sold on credit with a security interest taken in the equipment by each of the respective sellers. Which of the following is correct?

    a. The security interests of all of the sellers remain valid and will take priority even against good faith purchasers for value, despite the fact that resales were contemplated.
    b. The baseball equipment is inventory in the hands of all the parties concerned.
    c. Milo's security interest is automatically perfected since Milo qualifies as a purchase money secured party.
    d. Milo and the distributors must file a financing statement or take possession of the baseball equipment in order to perfect their security interests.

CHAPTER 30   SECTION 6   PAGE 533

---

    2. Therefore, a manufacturer in a non-consumer commercial transaction must file or possess the collateral. There is no automatic perfection as there is for a PMSI in CONSUMER goods. (T)

    3. A bona fide purchaser (BFP) for value has priority over subordinate lien creditors, but not senior lien creditors.

    4. A lien creditor, who has filed first, has priority over a secured party. (T) (See IV, A, 2.)

C.   There are two main exceptions to the above rules.

The candidate must commit to memory the two exceptions to the priority rules.

    1. The Buyer in the Ordinary Course of Business:

Secured Transactions: UCC Article 9   75

The bank has a security interest in the inventory of stoves at Joe's Appliance Store. Joe sells a stove to Fred, a consumer, and Fred knows about the bank's security interest. If Joe defaults on the inventory loan, the bank cannot take Fred's stove. Fred is a buyer in the ordinary course of business and beats the bank's perfected interest. (TTT) However, if Fred knew about Joe's default, then the bank wins.

NOVEMBER 1992 # 49

On July 8, Ace, a refrigerator wholesaler, purchased 50 refrigerators. This comprised Ace's entire inventory and was financed under an agreement with Rome Bank that gave Rome a security interest in all refrigerators on Aces's premises, all future-acquired refrigerators, and the proceeds of sales. On July 12, Rome filed a financing statement that adequately identified the collateral. On August 15, Ace sold one refrigerator to Cray for personal use and four refrigerators to Zone Co. for its business. Which of the following statements is correct?

a. The refrigerators sold to Zone will be subject to Rome's security interest.
b. **The refrigerator sold to Cray will not be subject to Rome's security interest.**
c. The security interest does not include the proceeds from the sale of the refrigerators to Zone.
d. The security interest may not cover after-acquired property even if the parties agree.

CHAPTER 30   SECTION 6   PAGE 533

---

2. The Consumer to Consumer Transaction

If Jane sells to Sally, her neighbor, a stove at garage sale, Sally may be able to defeat a perfected security interest after Jane's defaults on the bank loan. It does not matter that the creditor has a PMSI in consumer goods. The only way the bank can defeat Sally is if Sally had knowledge (constructive or actual) of the bank's interest. (TTT) Therefore, the bank should <u>file</u> its interest! In this way, Sally will have constructive knowledge of the prior secured interest.

May 1991 # 60

Wine purchased a computer using the proceeds of a loan from MJC Finance

Company. Wine gave MJC a security interest in the computer. Wine executed a security agreement and financing statement, which was filed by MJC. Wine used the computer to monitor Wine's personal investments. Later, Wine sold the computer to Jacobs, for Jacobs' family use. Jacobs was unaware of MJC's security interest. Wine now is in default under the MJC loan. May MJC repossess the computer from Jacobs?

    a.   No, because Jacobs was unaware of the MJC security interest.
    b.   No, because Jacobs intended to use the computer for family or household use.
    c.   **Yes, because MJC's security interest was perfected before Jacobs' purchase.**
    d.   Yes, because Jacobs' purchase of the computer made Jacobs personally liable to MJC.

CHAPTER 30   SECTION 6   PAGE 535

V.   Rights and Duties of the Debtors, Creditors and Third Parties (BFPs)

Default is not defined in the UCC, nor is the definition tested on the CPA Exam. Default is defined by the security agreement (the contract).

    A.   Creditor (Secured Party)

        1.   At default, the secured party has several options. The secured party may reduce the claim to judgment, sell the collateral and apply the proceeds to the debt, or take possession of the collateral without judicial process. (TTT)

November 1992 # 50

Under the UCC Secured Transactions Article, if a debtor is in default under a payment obligation secured by goods, the secured party has the right to

	Peacefully repossess the goods without judicial process	Reduce the claim to a judgment	Sell the goods and apply the proceeds toward the debt
a.	**Yes**	**Yes**	**Yes**

> | | | | |
> |---|---|---|---|
> | b. | No | Yes | Yes |
> | c. | Yes | Yes | No |
> | d. | Yes | No | Yes |
>
> CHAPTER 30   SECTION 8   PAGE 538

      2. After foreclosure, the risk of loss remains with the debtor, to the extent of any deficiency in the insurance coverage. (T)

      3. If the collateral is in consumer goods, the secured party has rights at the foreclosure sale. (T)

      4. The secured party may ask the debtor for any deficiency. (T)

  B. Debtor's Rights

      1. The debtor has redemption rights which can be lost at the end of the sale. (T)

      2. The debtor can request that the secured party sell the collateral. (T)

      3. The secured party must file, for the debtor, a termination statement one month after final payment. (T)

  C. Third Party Rights (BFP)

      1. The BFP, for value, takes free from subordinate liens or interests. (TTT) The BFP by definition must not have knowledge of the subordinate interest. Therefore, that particular creditor should have filed.

VI. Foreclosure Order

The general rules of order are: (TT)

  A. Expenses of the Foreclosure Sale (e.g. attorney and accountant fees)

  B. The Debt

  C. Subordinate Interests

  D. Surplus/Deficiency to the Debtor

78   Business Law and the CPA Exam

November 1993 # 53

In what order are the following obligations paid after a secured creditor rightfully sells the debtor's collateral after repossession?

        I.   Debt owed to any junior security holder.
        II. Secured party's reasonable sale expenses.
        III. Debt owed to the secured party.

  a.   I, II, III.
  b.   II, I, III.
  c.   II, III, I.
  d.   III, II, I.

CHAPTER 30 SECTION 8   PAGES 542

ESSAY QUESTIONS

MAY, 1981 NUMBER 3
CONSIGNMENT SALE

Issues Tested:

    I.   Consignment Under Article 2
    II. Secured Interest

The AICPA rarely tests on consignments. A consignment is a transaction where the owner of the goods (the consignor) delivers the goods to the consignee. The consignee sells the goods, passes title to the buyer, and remits the purchase price, minus commissions, to the consignor.

Article 2 treats the consignment as a "Sale or Return" with title in the hands of the consignee, unless the consignor complies with the requirements of Article 9.

NOVEMBER, 1983 NUMBER 2
SECURED CONSUMER TRANSACTIONS

Issues Tested:

    I.   PMSI in Consumer Goods

II. Priority

A lender has automatic perfection with a PMSI in consumer goods. The purchase money lender has a 10-day grace period in order to put other parties on notice of his/her secured interest. Without the filing, other parties could defeat the lender's interest.

NOVEMBER, 1984 NUMBER 4
COMPUTER AND STEREO SALES

Issues Tested:

    I.   Attachment
    II.   Consumer-to-Consumer Exception
    III. Entrustment (Article 2)

Tom Sauer purchased a computer and a stereo from Zen Sounds, Inc. for personal use. With regard to the computer, Sauer signed an installment purchase note and a security agreement. Under the terms of the note Sauer was to pay $100 down and $50 a month for 20 months. The security agreement included a description of the computer. However, Zen did not file a financing statement. Sauer paid $800 cash for the stereo.

Two months later, Sauer sold the computer to Ralph for $600 cash. Ralph purchased the computer for personal use without knowledge of Zen's security interest.

Three months later, Sauer brought the stereo back to Zen for repair. Inadvertently, one of Zen's sales persons sold the stereo to Ned, a buyer in the ordinary course of business.

REQUIRED:

Answer the following, setting forth reasons for any conclusions stated.

    1.   Did Zen fulfill the requirements necessary for the attachment and perfection of its security interest in the computer?

    2.   Will Ralph take the computer free of Zen's security interest?

    3.   Between Sauer and Ned, who has title to the stereo?

ANSWER:

Zen has done all it needs to in order to attach its secured interest to the computer. Zen has a written security agreement, and Sauer has signed the agreement. The agreement does describe the computer. Therefore, Zen has attached.

However, Zen did not file its security agreement. Ralph will take free of Zen's interest. This is an exception to the priority rules (see above IV,C,2). The Sauer-to-Ralph transaction is the "Consumer-to-Consumer" exception. Zen would have defeated Ralph, if Zen had filed the security agreement.

Ned has good title to the stereo, although Zen did not have title to the stereo. This is the "Entrustment Rule" under Article 2. Normally, a transferor can only transfer the title the transferor has. However, a merchant who deals in the goods of that kind of transaction can pass on better (here good) title. Although the facts provided by the AICPA are not clear, Zen probably deals in the sale of used/repaired stereos.

Sauer has two options. First, he can attack Ned's title by claiming that Zen is not a merchant of used/repaired stereos. This argument probably will not work. So Sauer must sue Zen.

MAY, 1988 NUMBER 4
PURCHASE MONEY SECURITY INTEREST

Issues Tested:

    I.   Types of PMSIs
    II.   Priority
    III. The Buyer in the Ordinary Course of Business Exception

A creditor can have a PMSI if the creditor is a retail store that lends money to a customer so that the customer can buy the creditor's merchandise. This is not a credit card transaction. If Sears lends money so a customer can afford furniture, Sears can receive a PMSI. The other example is if a bank lent money to the customer for the purchase of the furniture.

Such a creditor has automatic perfection with a PMSI in consumer (furniture) goods. The secured creditor can beat other lien creditors if the secured creditor files the PMSI in consumer goods within 10 days of possession. Generally, the time of filing or perfection will rank the priority of secured parties.

The main exception the AICPA will test on is the "buyer in the ordinary course of business." If Sears had a inventory loan on the furniture, the consumer would beat the security interest of the lender of the inventory. The consumer would win even if the consumer <u>knew</u> of the inventory loan. The secured lender would defeat the claim of the consumer if the consumer knew of the default.

NOVEMBER, 1991 NUMBER 5
ATTACHMENT

Issues Tested:

    I.   Attachment
    II.   Priority

Attachment of collateral requires that:

1. the security agreement must be in writing, describe the collateral, and be signed by the debtor.

2. the creditor must give value.

3. the debtor must have rights in the collateral.

If the creditor does not follow these requirements, he/she could lose his/her priority possession.

MAY, 1992 NUMBER 5
PRIORITY RULES

Issues Tested:

    I.   Priority Rules
    II.   Buyer in the Ordinary Course of Business Exception
    III. Holder in Due Course
    IV. Negotiability of an Instrument

A PMSI in inventory is not perfected unless the interest is filed. There is no automatic perfection. Again, the AICPA tests on the "buyer in the ordinary course of business." The buyer will defeat the creditor even if the buyer knew of the security interest.

An excellent place for the AICPA to test on Article 3 rule is in the note that is secured by Article 9 collateral.

LONG OBJECTIVE QUESTIONS
MAY 1995, NUMBER 3b

Issues Tested:

    I.   Elements of Attachment

II. Filing of Financing Statement as a Method of Perfection
III. Purchase Money Security Interest and the Priority Rules
IV. Buyer in the Ordinary Course of Business Exception

NOVEMBER, 1995 NUMBER 5
CPA REVIEW OF A NOTE

Issue Tested:

I. Priority Rules

Suretyship-Guarantor/ Debtor-Creditor

I. Elements of a Surety Relationships

In this legal relationship a promise is made to a creditor to pay the debts of a debtor by a third party (surety or guarantor). The candidate should be aware of the potential confusion between a surety and a guarantor.

A. Guarantor

A GUARANTOR only guarantees the debtor's debt.

1. Secondary Liability

The Guarantor is only secondarily liable (see UCC Article 3) on the debtor's obligation. This means the creditor must have attempted to collect from the debtor before the guarantor is liable. (T)

2. Statute of Frauds

The guarantor's promise to the creditor must be in writing. (T)

3. Exception to the Statute of Frauds—"Main Purpose Doctrine"

If the "Main Purpose" of the third party's promise to pay debtor's obligation is to benefit the third party (guarantor) him/herself (e.g. manufacturer guarantees the obligations of an important supplier), then an oral promise will be enforceable. (T)

May 1981 #39

Overall, Inc., owns 100% of the stock of Controlled Corporation, each being a separate entity. Overall telephoned the Factory Supply Company and ordered $400 of miscellaneous merchandise. Overall told Factory to ship the supplies to Controlled and Overall would pay for them. Factory did so and now seeks recovery of the price or damages. Which of the following is correct?

a. Overall is a surety.
b. **The Statute of Frauds will not bar Factory from recovering from Overall.**
c. Controlled is the principal debtor.
d. Overall and Controlled are jointly and severally liable on the contract.

CHAPTER 17   SECTION 2   PAGES 286-287
CHAPTER 31   SECTION 2   PAGE 553-554

B. Surety

1. A SURETY is primarily liable on the debtor's obligation. (T)

November 1989 #20

Burns borrowed $240,000 from Dollar Bank as additional working capital for his business. Dollar required that the loan be collateralized to the extent of 20%, and that an acceptable surety for the entire amount be obtained. Surety Co. agreed to act as surety on the loan and Burns pledged $48,000 of negotiable bearer bonds. Burns defaulted. Which of the following statements is correct?

a. Dollar must first liquidate the collateral before it can proceed against Surety.
b. **Surety is liable in full immediately upon default by Burns, but will be entitled to the collateral upon satisfaction of the debt.**
c. Dollar must first proceed against Burns and obtain a judgement before it can proceed against the collateral.
d. Surety may proceed against Burns for the full amount of the loan even if Surety settles with Dollar for a lower amount.

CHAPTER 31   SECTION 2   PAGE 553

2. A surety's promise is <u>not</u> required to be in writing under the Statute of Frauds.

Therefore, the surety's oral promise is enforceable. (T)

3. Consideration is <u>not</u> required to enforce the surety contract if the surety contract arose at the same time as the original debtor-creditor contract. (WTT)

November 1982 #24

Knott obtained a loan of $10,000 from Charles on January 1, 1982 payable on April 15, 1982. At the time of the loan, Beck became a noncompensated surety thereon by written agreement. On April 15, 198, Knott was unable to pay and wrote to Charles requesting an extension of time. Charles made no reply, but did not take any immediate action to recover. On May 30, 1982 Charles demanded payment from Knott and, failing to collect from him, proceeded against Beck. Based upon the facts stated,

    a. Charles was obligated to obtain a judgement against Knott returned unsatisfied before he could collect from Beck.
    b. Beck is released from his surety obligation because Charles granted Knott an extension of time.
    c. Charles may recover against Beck, despite the fact that Beck was a noncompensated surety.
    d. Beck is released because Charles delayed in proceeding against Knott.

CHAPTER N/A   PAGE N/A

---

4. No compensation is required to hold the surety liable. (WTT)

II. Defenses of the Surety/Guarantor

    A. Generally the SURETY/GUARANTOR can use the defenses that the debtor has against the creditor,

        1. Duress (T)

        2. Fraud (T)

        3. Illegality (T)

        4. Forgery (T)

86 Business Law and the CPA Exam

        5. Lack of Consideration (T)

    but <u>not</u>

        1. Incapacity (TT)

        2. Bankruptcy (TT)

        3. Death (TT)

    These defenses are too personal in nature.

    B. The surety/guarantor can use his/her own defenses against the creditors. (T)

        1. If the debtor committed fraud against the creditor and the creditor knew of the fraud, the surety/guarantor has a defense. (TTT)

III. Release of the Surety/Guarantor (also see Defenses)

    A. Tender of payment or payment by the debtor. (TTT)

    B. Impairment or release of collateral by the creditor. (TT)

    C. Delegation from one debtor to another. (T)

    D. The creditor does not exhaust his/her legal collection remedies against the debtor. (T) This only releases the guarantor since he/she is only secondarily liable.

    E. Release of the debtor by the creditor releases the surety/guarantor. (T)

    F. Material modification of the original debtor/creditor contract (e.g. the extension of payments) releases the surety/guarantor. (T) This is not so if the surety is compensated. (T)

IV. Rights of the Surety/Guarantor

    A. Subrogation

        1. Once the surety pays the debtor's obligation, the surety is subrogated to creditor's rights. (TTT)

Suretyship-Guarantor/Debtor-Creditor 87

> May 1981 # 38
>
> Reginald, who is insolvent, defaulted on a loan upon which Jayne was the surety. Edward, the creditor, demanded payment from Jayne of the amount owed by Reginald. The loan was also secured by a mortgage which Edward has the right to foreclose. Which of the following is Jayne's best legal course of action?
>
>   a.   Seek specific performance by Reginald.
>   b.   Refuse to pay until Reginald has been petitioned into bankruptcy and the matter has been decided by the trustee in bankruptcy.
>   **c.**   **Pay Edward and resort to the subrogation rights to the collateral.**
>   d.   Refuse to pay because Edward must first resort to the collateral.
>
> CHAPTER 31   SECTION 2   PAGE 555

    2.   In fact, the surety, after subrogation, can go after the collateral. (T)

    3.   Bankruptcy does not change the right of subrogation. The surety is like a creditor in bankruptcy. (T)

    4.   Subrogation is an independent contract right. The surety has every right to subrogate even if the other co-sureties do not subrogate. (T)

B.   Contribution (from co-sureties)

    1.   If a co-surety pays more than the proportionate share, the surety can demand "contribution" from his/her co-sureties. (TTT)

> November 1993 # 25
>
> Nash, Owen, and Polk are co-sureties with maximum liabilities of $40,000, $60,000 and $80,000, respectively. The amount of the loan on which they have agreed to act as co-sureties is $180,000. Nash paid the lender $36,000 in full settlement of all claims against Nash, Owen, and Polk. The total amount that Nash may recover from Owen and Polk is
>
>   a. $0   b. $24,000   **c. $28,000**   d. $140,000
>
> CHAPTER 31   SECTION 2   PAGE 555

2. However, the surety only shares in this cost in proportion to the maximum amount that the surety agreed to pay. (WT)

3. Co-surety must perform even if the other co-sureties will not. (T)

C. Reimbursement (indemnification) by the debtor.

1. The surety has the right to ask for reimbursement from the debtor for the amounts paid to the creditor by the surety, and for expenses. (T)

2. When the surety makes a voluntary payment to the creditor, then the surety is not entitled to reimbursement from the debtor. (T)

D. Exoneration

1. The surety can demand that the creditor go against the debtor. (WTT)

November 1986 #28

Queen paid Pax & Co. to become the surety on a loan which Queen obtained from Squire. The loan is due and Pax wishes to compel Queen to pay Squire. Pax has not made any payments to Squire in its capacity as Queen's surety. Pax will be most successful if it exercises its right to

a. reimbursement (indemnification).
b. contribution.
c. exoneration.
d. subrogation.

CHAPTER N/A   PAGE N/A

V. Debtor-Creditor

A. Liens - Mechanic's Lien is a creditor remedy for the improvement of REAL property. An Artisan's Lien is a creditor remedy for the improvement of PERSONAL property. The creditor can sell the property in order to satisfy the debt. (T)

B. Writ of Garnishment- Federal social security benefits are exempt from garnishments by creditors. (T)

ESSAY QUESTIONS

You should not confuse the surety with a guarantor. The surety is primarily liable, while the guarantor only guarantees the contract. The creditor must exhaust all his/her legal remedies before the creditor can demand guarantor performance. The surety relationship does not have to be in writing. (However, many states do require a writing under the state's Statute of Frauds.)

NOVEMBER, 1980 NUMBER 3a
SURETY/GUARANTOR CONTRACT

Issues Tested:

    I.   Primary Liability
    II.   Co-surety
    III. Release

The surety is primarily liable to the creditor. The creditor can demand immediate payment from the surety for the failure of the debtor to perform. If there is a release of one co-surety, then the remaining co-sureties are also released.

SURETY/GUARANTOR CONTRACT

Issues Tested:

    I.   Writing
    II.   Notification
    III. Defenses
    IV. Release

The surety, who is primarily liable to the creditor, does not require a writing. The guarantor, who only guarantees payment, requires a writing.

Since the guarantor is not primarily liable, the creditor must first exhaust his/her legal remedies against the debtor before the creditor can demand the guaranteed payment from the guarantor. While it is true that a guarantor can use some of the defenses of the debtor, the guarantor cannot use all of these defenses. If the defense is personal in nature, then the guarantor cannot use the defense. For instance, bankruptcy and minority are types of defenses that a guarantor or a surety cannot use.

Finally, a guarantor/surety will be released if there is a modification of the original debtor/creditor relationship. A modification that increases the term for the original loan at a higher interest rate is such an example. The law releases the surety/guarantor since it would be unfair to materially increase the burden of these parties by increasing the time the surety/guarantor is liable.

BANKRUPTCY

Bankruptcy should be in an area of the law that the AICPA would be expected to test in earnest. However, this expectation is not totally accurate. Bankruptcy only occupies a portion of the Debtor-Creditor section. One would expect a heavier testing, since an accountant may be the first to reach the realization that bankruptcy is the only practical debtor remedy for his/her client. Also, the bankruptcy section would seem to be, and is, a prime station for testing the math skills of the accountant, as the estate and the distribution must be calculated.

Still, the candidate should take special note that the bankruptcy laws have changed. This change is the first statutory change since 1978. Prior to 1994, the post 1978 changes were judicial changes. While the 1978 statute has been generally pro-debtor, the judicial decisions have been more pro-creditor. The CPA Exam has tested in the past that the 1978 Act increased the debtor exemptions and eliminated certain chapters in bankruptcy. (T) As of October of 1997, more pro-creditor changes have been discussed. These changes are in response to growing number of personal filings.

The candidate should commit to memory the chapters in Bankruptcy:

Chapter 7	Liquidation	(Tested often)
Chapter 11	Reorganization	(Tested often)
Chapter 13	Repayment	(Not tested often)
Chapter 12	Farms	(Rarely, if ever, tested)

I. Liquidation Proceedings (Chapter 7)

    A. Filing the Petition

        1. Who can file and who cannot file. (TT)

            a. Individual persons, partnerships and corporations may file.

b. Railroads, insurance companies, banks, savings and loan associations and credit unions cannot file Chapter 7. They must resort to other state debtor remedies such as receiverships.

1. Voluntary Bankruptcy

   a. A debtor does not have to show that he/she is insolvent to file for bankruptcy. In fact, the debtor only needs only show that he/she owes somebody. The issues of insolvency becomes important for other matters. The amount of the debt, therefore, is irrelevant. (TTT) See *In Re Johns-Manville Corp.*, Chapter 32, Section 3

May 1983 #21

A voluntary bankruptcy proceeding is available to

a. all debtors provided they are insolvent.
b. debtors only if the overwhelming preponderance of creditors has not petitioned for and obtained a receivership pursuant to state law.
c. corporations only if a reorganization has been attempted and failed.
d. most debtors even if they are not insolvent.

CHAPTER 32   SECTION 1   PAGES 559-560
CHAPTER 32   SECTION 3   PAGES 570-571

---

   b. A husband and wife may make a joint filing. (T)

2. Involuntary Bankruptcy

   a. Creditors can throw a debtor into bankruptcy if the debtor is not paying his/her debts as due and the creditors meet other statutory guidelines. (TT)

   b. If the debtor does not contest the involuntary filing, then the court can grant an "Order for Relief." (T)

   c. The debtor can fight the involuntary filing, win dismissal, and receive his/her costs and attorney fees. (TT)

   d. The court can require the creditors to post bond. (T)

e. The candidate should study the limit requirements for a creditor to file involuntary bankruptcy. If there are twelve or more creditors, then three of those creditors must have unsecured claims totaling at least $5,000 in order to file the involuntary remedy. If there are fewer than twelve, then only one creditor must be the above limits. (TT)

B. Automatic Stay

This is the main reason to file bankruptcy. The automatic stay, in voluntary and involuntary bankruptcy, suspends nearly all creditor collection efforts. (TTT)

November 1993 # 27

The filing of an involuntary bankruptcy petition under the Federal Bankruptcy Code

a. terminates liens on exempt property.
b. terminates all security interests in property in the bankruptcy estate.
c. stops the debtor from incurring new debts.
d. stops the enforcement of judgement liens against property in the bankruptcy estate.

CHAPTER 32   SECTION 2   PAGE 562

C. Property of the Estate

1. Interests in property, such as gifts, inheritance, divorce settlements and life insurance proceeds to which the debtor becomes entitled within 180 days after filing may become part of the estate. (TTT)

November 1990 # 35

A bankrupt party who filed voluntarily and received a discharge in bankruptcy under the provisions of Chapter 7 of the Federal Bankruptcy Code

a. may obtain another voluntary discharge in bankruptcy under Chapter 7 after five years.
b. will receive a discharge of any and all debts owed.
c. is precluded from owning or operating a similar business for two years.

> d. must surrender for distribution to the creditors any amount received as an inheritance if received within 180 days after filing the petition.
>
> CHAPTER 32   SECTION 2   PAGES 562-563

D. Creditor's Meeting and Claims

A PMSI in equipment filed within 10 days has a superior claim. (T)

E. Exemptions

The CPA Exam cannot test too extensively in this area. The Bankruptcy Code allows each state to choose the state's own exemptions or the Bankruptcy Code's. Since this is a multistate exam, the examiners will not test the candidate on their state's exemptions. However, the candidate should be aware of the exemptions. The CPA Exam can require the candidate to calculate the estate with a given set of exemptions. The Bankruptcy Act of 1994 has changed some of the exemption limits. This act adjusts these limits in accordance with the Consumer Price Index.

F. Trustee

1. The trustee can accept or reject executory contracts (e.g. a lease). (TT)

2. A CPA can be a trustee and the tax preparer. (T)

3. The trustee has PREFERENCE power. If the debtor "preferred" certain creditors before the filing, the trustee has the power to recover these payments. The CPA exam tests on the requirements.

    a. The preference must be made by an INSOLVENT debtor for a PREEXISTING debt transferred within 90 days of the filing. (TTT)

> November 1993 # 30
>
> Which of the following transfers by a debtor, within ninety days of filing for bankruptcy, could be set aside as a preferential payment?
>
> a. Making a gift to charity.
> b. Paying a business utility bill.

> c. Borrowing money from a bank secured by giving a mortgage on business property.
> **d. Prepaying an installment loan on inventory.**
>
> CHAPTER 32   SECTION 2   PAGE 565-566

    b. A consumer to debtor transfer for $6,000 is <u>not</u> considered to be a preference. (T)

4. The trustee is the representative in bankruptcy. The trustee can sue and be sued. (T)

G. Distribution

The candidate must know the order of DISTRIBUTION. (TTT)

1. Secured Creditors

The secured creditor can later become an unsecured creditor. For instance, if the secured creditor forecloses on the collateral, but does not receive full satisfaction, then he/she becomes a unsecured creditor for the deficiency. Therefore, it is possible that a secured creditor may not get fully paid. (TTT)

> May 1981 # 43
>
> If a secured party's claim exceeds the value of the collateral of a bankrupt, he/she will be paid the total amount realized from the sale of the security and will
>
> a. not have any claim for the balance.
> **b. become a general creditor for the balance.**
> c. retain a secured creditor status for the balance.
> d. be paid the balance only after all general creditors are paid.
>
> CHAPTER 32   SECTION 2   PAGE 566

2. Unsecured Creditors

The candidate should understand that each of the following classes must be satisfied before payment can begin with the next class. If there is not enough to satisfy a particular class, then that class shares proportionately within its class. (TTT)

    a. Administrative expenses (trustee, attorney, accountant, court fees) are paid first. (TT)

    b. Expenses in the ordinary course of business (involuntary bankruptcy)

    c. Unpaid wages, etc.

    d. Unpaid pension contributions

    e. Certain claims of farmers and fishermen

    f. Certain consumer deposits

    g. Certain taxes and penalties (T)

    h. Claims of general creditors (remember the deficiency of the secured creditor).

H. Discharge

    1. Non-Dischargeable Debts tested include:

        a. Alimony and child support (T)

        The 1994 Act places these payments in higher priority over unpaid taxes and the payments are excepted from the automatic stay.

        b. Money obtained by fraud (T)

    2. Denial of Discharge

        a. Debtor's fraudulent concealment, destruction, or failure to persevere the financial records. (TT)

Bankruptcy 97

> May 1984 #16
>
> A debtor will be denied a discharge in bankruptcy if the debtor
>
> a. failed to timely list a portion of his/her debts.
> b. **unjustifiably failed to preserve his/her books and records which could have been used to ascertain the debtor's financial condition.**
> c. has negligently made preferential transfers to favored creditors within 90 days of the filing of the bankruptcy petition.
> d. has committed several willful and malicious acts which resulted in bodily injury to others.
>
> CHAPTER 32   SECTION 2   PAGE 569

II. Reorganization (Chapter 11)

Most of the above rules of Chapter 7 apply to Chapter 11. The unique rules of Chapter 11 are listed below.

A. Chapter 11 is not liquidation. The debtor remains in possession of his/her assets. (TT)

> November 1993 # 33
>
> A reorganization under Chapter 11 of the Federal Bankruptcy Code requires all of the following except the
>
> a. **liquidation of the debtor.**
> b. the filing of a reorganization plan.
> c. confirmation for each class of claims to accept the reorganization plan.
>
> CHAPTER 32   SECTION 3   PAGE 571

B. Those debtors eligible in Chapter 7 are also eligible in Chapter 11. The exclusions are stockbrokers/commodities brokers. Railroads are now included, but savings and loans are still not covered. (TT)

C. Chapter 11 requires the court to create a committee for unsecured creditor claims. (TT)

D. Chapter 11 can be voluntary and involuntary. One creditor can file if there are fewer than 12 creditors (TT) In addition, a debtor can object to the filing but only if the debtor is not insolvent under the Bankruptcy (not paying its debts as they become due). (T)

E. Creditor confirmation of the plan is not required. The court can use its "Cram-Down" authority. (T)

ESSAY QUESTIONS

MAY, 1986 NUMBER 5
DISCHARGE IN CHAPTER 7 (LIQUIDATION)

Issue Tested:

I. Denial or Revocation of Discharge

The candidate should not confuse the exceptions of discharge with the general denial of discharge and the revocation of discharge. This essay question tested on the denial of discharge and the revocation of discharge.

The debtor will be denied discharge for the following acts:

1. Refusal to obey a lawful Bankruptcy Court order.
2. Fraudulent concealment or destruction of financial records.
3. Concealment or destruction of property with the intent of hindering, delaying or defrauding a creditor.
4. Failure to satisfactorily explain the loss of assets.
5. Waiver.

The Bankruptcy Court will revoke the discharge upon petition of a creditor or the trustee. The revocation petition must be within one year of the discharge. The Court will grant the revocation if the debtor acted fraudulently or dishonestly during the bankruptcy proceedings.

NOVEMBER, 1987 NUMBER 3
PRIORITY IN INVOLUNTARY BANKRUPTCY

Issues Tested:

I. Requirements for Involuntary Filing
II. Trustee Eligibility

III. The Estate
IV. Priority

For an involuntary filing, creditors must have noncontingent, unsecured claims of $5,000 or more. If there are 12 or more creditors, 3 of them must join in the petition. If there are less than 12 creditors, one may file.

An accountant may be appointed a trustee.

The estate consists of all tangible and intangible property in which the debtor has a legal/equitable interest or claim. The property can be outside the court's federal circuit/district. The estate also includes property that may be exempt. The estate consists of property that the debtor received by gift, inheritance, or divorce/insurance settlement within 180 days from the filing of the petition (the AICPA tests on the 180-day rule extensively in the multiple choice and essay questions).

The student should generally know the order of distribution among the following classes.

1. Secured Creditors
2. Cost and expenses of the estate (accountant, attorney and trustee fees)
3. Ordinary business expenses (in an involuntary proceeding before the election of the trustee)
4. Certain unpaid wages
5. Certain unpaid pension contributions
6. Certain farmer and fisherman claims
7. Limited consumer deposits
8. Taxes and penalties
9. General unsecured creditors

Each class must be satisfied before the next class can be paid. If there is not enough to satisfy the whole class, then the distribution must be pro-rata within the class.

MAY, 1989 NUMBER 2
INVOLUNTARY FILING

Issues Tested:

I. Involuntary Requirements
II. Trustee Preference Power
III. Denial of Discharge

For the requirements of the involuntary filing, see November, 1987 or the multiple choice section.

The trustee can avoid certain debtor transfers if the debtor favored one creditor over another creditor. The trustee must show:

1. The transfer was done by insolvent debtor for a preexisting debt,
2. The transfer was made within 90 days before the date of bankruptcy filing,
3. This transfer allowed the creditor to receive more than the creditor would have received in the bankruptcy proceeding.

For denial of discharge see May, 1986. The Court can deny a debt from discharge if the debtor obtains the money by fraud.

MAY, 1990 NUMBER 2
TRUSTEE'S PREFERENCE POWER

Issues Tested:

I. Nondischargeable Debts
II. Trustee's Preference Power

Claims not dischargeable include:

1. Back taxes within 3 years of bankruptcy
2. Claims for money the debtor obtained by fraud
3. Unscheduled claims
4. Breaches of fiduciary duties
5. Intentional tort claims
6. Alimony and child support
7. Injury claims based on debtor's drunk driving
8. Student loans (unless debtor proves undue hardship)
9. Certain luxury goods/services claims
10. Certain consumer credit advances

See May, 1989 for trustee preference power.

MAY, 1992 NUMBER 4
INVOLUNTARY BANKRUPTCY

Issues Tested:

I. Involuntary Filing Requirements
II. Relief from the Automatic Stay
III. Trustee Preference Power

For the involuntary requirements see November, 1987.

The automatic stay is a major reason the debtor files for bankruptcy. However, the automatic stay is one of the major reasons that a creditor perfects his/her security interest under Article 9 of the UCC. The secured creditor may not be adequately protected and may apply for relief from the automatic stay. The creditor may petition to the court to require the debtor to provide more collateral or continue payments on the secured collateral. The creditor may request possession of the collateral if the debt exceeds the fair market value of the collateral.

However, the creditor will be liable for actual damages if the creditor violates the automatic stay. Even if the creditor can take possession of the collateral and foreclose, the creditor will be an unsecured creditor for the deficiency.

For trustee preference power see May, 1989.

LONG OBJECTIVE QUESTIONS
NOVEMBER, 1995 NUMBER 3a
INVOLUNTARY BANKRUPTCY

Issues Tested

   I.   Creditor Priority
   II. Preferential Transfers

AGENCY

I. Formation and Duties

   A. Nature and Formation

      1. Consensual

The agency relationship does <u>not</u> require consideration. Therefore, the relationship does not have to be contractual. However, the agency relationship must be consensual. (TT)

May 1992 # 8

A principal and agent relationship requires a

   a. written agreement.
   b. Power of Attorney.
   c. meeting of the minds and consent to act.
   d. specified consideration.

CHAPTER 33   SECTION 2   PAGE 587

---

      2. Agency Coupled with an Interest

Here, the agent receives the benefit of the relationship. The agent is said to have a beneficial interest. The mere fact that an agent may be paid or receive a commission is not enough to create this type of interest. If "agency coupled with an interest" exists, then the relationship is irrevocable. (TT)

      3. The Equal Dignity Rule

The creation of the agency relationship does not normally require a writing.

But under each state's Equal Dignity Rule, if the underlying transaction requires a writing under the Statute of Frauds, then the agent's authority must also be in writing. The AICPA tests more on the one-year rule and land, but not the UCC's $500 limit on the sale of goods. Do not pick the UCC answer if either of the other two are present. (TT)

May 1985 #1

Wok Corp. has decided to expand the scope of its business. In this connection, it contemplates engaging several agents. Which of the following agency relationships is within the Statute of Frauds and thus should be contained in a signed writing?

a. A sales agency where the agent normally will sell goods which have a value in excess of $500.
b. An irrevocable agency.
c. An agency which is of indefinite duration which is terminable upon one month's notice.
d. An agency for the forthcoming calendar year which is entered into in mid-December of the prior year.

CHAPTER 33   SECTION 2   PAGE 587

---

4. Capacity

A minor can be an agent, but a minor does not have the capacity to be a principal.

B. Kinds of Agency Relationships

The AICPA does not directly test on the obvious relationships (principal/agent or employer/employee), but does test on the types of agency relationships that an accountant may encounter.

1. Independent Contractor

This is a growing area of the law. Most employers would like to call their employees INDEPENDENT CONTRACTORS to alleviate their tax withholding problems and reduce their legal liability exposure. The candidate should be familiar with the factors that aid in determination of the independent contractor status.

a. Control

There has been one question on CONTROL as a factor. (T)

November 1981 #15

The key characteristic of a servant is that

a.　his physical conduct is controlled or subject to the right of control by the employer.
b.　he is paid at an hourly rate as contrasted with the payment of a salary.
c.　he is precluded from making contracts for and on behalf of his/her employer.
d.　he lacks apparent authority to bind his employer.

CHAPTER 33   SECTION 1   PAGE 585

---

2. Agency by Estoppel (See later Apparent Authority)

3. Agency by Ratification (See later Ratification of Authority)

4. Power of Attorney

The CPA Exam tests more on "special" powers than "general" powers. One does not have to be an attorney to have the "power." The power will only exist for certain specific acts. The power is effective when signed and terminates at the death of the principal or the agent. (TT)

C. Duties

The AICPA does not test on the full range of the duties in an agency relationship. But certain duties are tested frequently.

1. Duties (Agent to Principal)

Generally these duties are fiduciary duties. (T)

a. Loyalty

The agent must not engage in conflicts of interest, nor compete against the principal without disclosure/consent. (TTT)

May 1991 # 9

Ogden Corp. hired Thorp as a sales representative for nine months at a salary of $3,000 per month plus 4% of sales. Which of the following statements is correct?

- a. **Thorp is obligated to act solely in Ogden's interest in matters concerning Ogden's business.**
- b. The agreement between Ogden and Thorp formed an agency coupled with an interest.
- c. Ogden does not have the power to dismiss Thorp during the nine-month period without cause.
- d. The agreement between Ogden and Thorp is not enforceable unless it is in writing and signed by Thorp.

CHAPTER 33   SECTION 3   PAGES 590-592

---

      b.   Notification

Under the rule of "Imputed Knowledge," everything the agent knows the principal is imputed to know. Therefore the agent has the duty to notify his/her principal. (TT)

2. Duties (Principal to Agent)

The AICPA rarely tests on these types of duties.

3. Remedies of the Principal or the Agent.

The AICPA rarely tests in this area.

I. Agency Authority, Ratification, Liability and Termination

    A. Authority

This is a very important area of this section (agency) and of the CPA Exam generally. Candidates should not enter the exam without a clear understanding of the different types of AUTHORITY. It is not enough to know the types but, also, their interrelationships and formations. For example, there are two basic types of authority—

actual and apparent. It is actual authority that has several subsets. With actual authority there are two main subcategories—expressed and implied. From there actual expressed authority is broken down into written and oral.

Therefore, Agency authority breaks down like this:

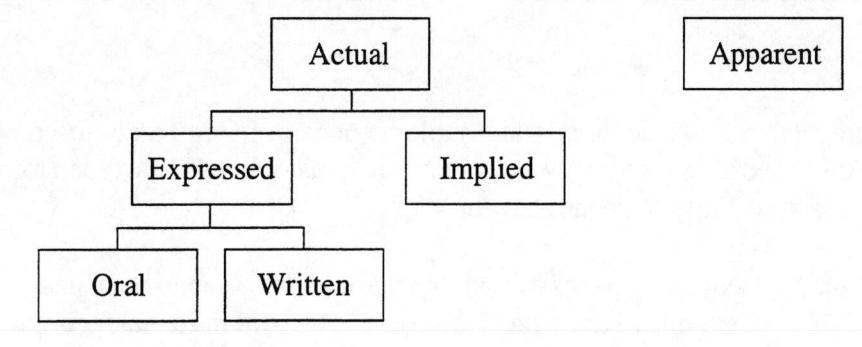

```
         Actual                    Apparent
        /      \
   Expressed   Implied
   /      \
 Oral    Written
```

1. Actual

   Not a prime area for testing.

2. Implied

   Implied authority flows from actual authority. In order to carry out his/her actual authority, an agent has certain "implied powers" from custom or necessity. (T)

3. Apparent Authority (a.k.a. Ostensible Authority or Agency by Estoppel).

   It is imperative that the candidate understand APPARENT AUTHORITY.

   a. Apparent authority is created when the principal does or does not do something that leads a third party to believe that the agent has the authority. (T)

   b. There is nothing the agent can do to create apparent authority. Therefore, the third party must be aware of the limitation of authority placed on the agent. (TT) In fact, to terminate apparent authority the principal must give the third party adequate actual notice of the termination. (TT) Questions (multiple choice or essay) concerning apparent authority should appear in situations where the principal has terminated the agent's actual authority or where the agent has exceeded his/her actual authority.

B. Ratification

If the agent has no actual authority or exceeds his/her actual authority, the principal

108   Business Law and the CPA Exam

can still accept (or ratify) his/her actions. Therefore, the AICPA tests on the elements of ratification. These elements include:

1. The principal must have full knowledge of all the material facts. (TT)

May 1985 # 2

Red entered into a contract with Maple on behalf of Gem, a disclosed principal. Red exceeded his authority in entering into the contract. In order for Gem to successfully ratify the contract with Maple,

- a. Gem must expressly communicate his intention to be bound.
- **b. Gem must have knowledge of the relevant material facts concerning the transaction.**
- c. Red must not have been a minor.
- d. Red must have acted reasonably and in Gem's best interest.

CHAPTER 33   SECTION 1   PAGES 601-602

---

2. The principal must have capacity. (T)

3. The principal must ratify the whole transaction.

4. The principal must accept before the third party withdraws. (T)

November 1984 # 15

Sol, an agent for May, made a contract with Simon which exceeded Sol's authority. If May wishes to hold Simon to the contract, May must prove that

- a. Sol was May's general agent even though Sol exceeded his authority.
- b. Sol believed he was acting within the scope of his authority.
- c. Sol was acting in the capacity of an agent for an undisclosed principal.
- **d. May ratified the contract before withdrawal from the contract by Simon.**

CHAPTER 33   SECTION 1   PAGES 601-602

5. The ratification can be done by expressed words or conduct, or by implication (e.g. accepting benefits). (TTT) Do not discuss reasonableness. (T)

C. Liability (Contract and Tort)

1. Contract

   This is a difficult area. The candidate must know the types of principals.

   - Disclosed Principal – existence and identity is known to third party.

   - Partially Disclosed Principal – existence, but no identity.

   - Undisclosed Principal – no existence and no identity (as if the third party is dealing with the agent only).

   a. The AICPA tests almost exclusively in the area of the undisclosed principal.

      1) If an agent works for an undisclosed principal (no existence, no identity), then the third party is said to be contracting with the agent. (T) In addition, the third party is not entitled to ratification or disclosure. (T)

      2) In fact, the agent has the right to enforce the contract. (T) An undisclosed principal cannot ratify a transaction if the agent goes beyond the scope of his/her employment. (T)

      3) This area is similar to contract liability under Article 3 of the UCC. Therefore no one is liable on the instrument (or by agency in contract) unless his/her name appears. (T)

      4) An agent also has implied powers when he/she represents an undisclosed principal. (T)

      5) With either the undisclosed principal or the partially disclosed principal, the third party can elect to hold either the agent or principal liable once the identity of the principal is known. (TTT)

May, 1984 # 12

Jim, an undisclosed principal, authorized Rick to act as his agent in securing a contract for the purchase of some plain white paper. Rick, without informing Sam that he was acting on behalf of a principal, entered into a contract with Sam to purchase the paper. If Jim repudiates the contract with Sam, which of the following is correct?

a. Rick will be released from his contractual obligations to Sam if he discloses Jim's identity.
b. **Upon learning that Jim is the principal, Sam may elect to hold either Jim or Rick liable on the contract.**
c. Rick may not enforce the contract against Sam.
d. Sam may obtain specific performance, compelling Jim to perform on the contract.

CHAPTER 33   SECTION 2   PAGE 603

2. Tort Liability

   This is a favorite area on the CPA Exam.

   a. An employer is liable for the torts of his/her employees, if the tort is committed within the scope of the employee's employment (e.g. *respondeat superior*). (TTT)

   b. Do not forget that an employee <u>is always</u> liable for his/her <u>own</u> torts. (TT)

   c. The principal/employer is not liable for the torts of independent contractors.

   d. An indemnity and hold harmless agreements between the employer/principal and the employee/agent are <u>not</u> binding on the injured third party. (WT)

November 1983 # 12

Ivy Corp. engaged Jones as a sales representative and assigned him to a route in southern Florida. Jones worked out of Ivy's main office and his duties, hours, and

Agency 111

routes were carefully controlled. The employment contract contained a provision which stated: "I, Jones, do hereby promise to hold the corporation harmless from any and all tort liability to third parties which may arise in carrying out my duties as an employee." On a sales call, Jones negligently dropped a case of hammers on the foot of Devlin, the owner of Devlin's Hardware. Which of the following statements is correct?

- a. Ivy has no liability to Devlin.
- **b. Although the exculpatory clause may be valid between Ivy and Jones, it does not affect Devlin's rights**
- c. Ivy is not liable to Devlin in any event, since Jones is an independent contractor.
- d. The exculpatory clause is totally invalid since it is against public policy.

CHAPTER N/A   SECTION N/A   PAGE N/A

D. Termination

1. The principal or the agent may have the power to terminate the relationship, but not the right. (TTT)

2. The relationship is automatically terminated by operation of law if the principal or the agent dies, goes insane, or because of impossibility or if the relationship becomes illegal. Also, no notice is required. (TTT)

3. Renunciation is termination by an act of the parties (the agent) and not by law. (T)

4. Agency "coupled, with an interest" is an example where the principal has the power, but not the right to terminate the relationship. (T)

5. Notice Requirements

If the agent has personally dealt with the third party (prior dealings), then actual termination notice by the principal is required. But if there is no actual prior dealing, then the principal needs only to give constructive (published) notice of the termination. (T)

> November 1987 # 25
>
> Dart Corp. dismissed Ritz as its general sales agent. Dart notified all of Ritz's known customers by letter. Bing Corp., a retail outlet located outside of Ritz's previously assigned sales territory, had never dealt with Ritz. However, Bing knew of Ritz as a result of various business contacts. After his dismissal, Ritz sold Bing goods, to be delivered by Dart, and received from Bing a cash deposit for 20% of the purchase price. It was not unusual for an agent in Ritz's previous position to receive cash deposits. In an action by Bing against Dart on the sales contract, Bing will:
>
>   **a.**   **win, because Dart's notice was inadequate to terminate Ritz's apparent authority.**
>   b.   win, because a principal is an insurer of an agent's acts.
>   c.   lose, because Ritz lacked any express or implied authority to make the contract.
>   d.   lose, because Ritz's conduct constituted a fraud for which Dart is not liable.
>
> **CHAPTER 33   SECTION 7   PAGES 613-614**

ESSAY QUESTIONS

The type of agency questions asked by AICPA in the essay exam are obvious. Apparent authority is the type of essay question you should expect on the exam. Another type of question asked in the last ten years is Agency Coupled with an Interest.

NOVEMBER, 1985 NUMBER 3b
TERMINATION OF AN AGENCY CONTRACT

Issues Tested:

    I.   Agency Coupled with an Interest
    II.   Termination of Agency Relationship
    III. Power vs. Right to Terminate Agency Relationship

An agency that is coupled with an interest is an irrevocable agency. The AICPA tests on this significance, but also on how this agency is created. In this type of agency, the relationship is created for the benefit of the agent. Do not confuse this with an agent having a monetary interest in the agency.

For example, a principal hires a real estate agent to sell a certain plot of land. First, the agency must be in writing in order to comply with the state's Equal Dignity Rule. Next, the agency is <u>not</u> an agency coupled with an interest. Although the agent has a monetary interest in the relationship, this agency is still revocable. Having a monetary interest (profits or commissions) alone will be not make the agency irrevocable.

The agent must receive a beneficial interest. The text provides an excellent example. If the principal owes the agent money, and the principal/debtor supplies the agent/creditor with the possession of the collateral, the agent/creditor has the authority to sell the collateral in the event of default. This is an agency coupled with an interest. The agent/creditor has a beneficial interest in that the collateral must be sold to satisfy the security interest. The principal/debtor cannot revoke the agency relationship.

Clearly if the AICPA tests in this area, the AICPA would not test on revocable agency. The essay for this question could be answered in a few sentences. Therefore, the CPA Exam will test on the more difficult areas.

Next, what happens if the principal revokes the agency? The CPA candidate should know that the principal generally has the <u>power</u> to terminate the agency, but <u>not</u> the <u>right</u>! An agent can be dismissed without cause. However, since the principal does not possess the right to terminate the agency, the principal will be liable for damages.

NOVEMBER, 1990 NUMBER 3
CONTRACT AND TORT LIABILITY

Issues Tested:

      I.   Undisclosed/partially disclosed principal
      II.   *Respondeat Superior*
      III. Apparent Authority
      IV. Notice of Termination

The AICPA wants the candidate to know the contract liability of the partially or undisclosed principal. When an agent contracts for an undisclosed principal with a third party, the third party believes that he/she is contracting with the agent. Once the third party learns of the existence and the identity of the principal, the third party must <u>choose</u> which of the two to sue. There is no joint liability in this situation.

For *respondeat superior*, see below.

If a third party has personally dealt with the agent, the principal owes the third party actual notice of the termination of authority. If the third has not personally dealt with the agent, then the principal must only provide constructive (e.g. published) notice of the termination. If the principal fails to provide the proper form of notice, then the principal will liable to the third party under apparent authority.

NOVEMBER, 1992 NUMBER 4
EMPLOYER'S LIABILITY IN TORT AND CONTRACT FOR EMPLOYEE'S ACTIONS

Issues Tested:

- I. Apparent Authority
- II. Implied Authority
- III. Agent's Duty of Loyalty
- IV. Imputed Knowledge
- V. *Respondeat Superior*

This question concerns the highly testable issues of apparent authority and *respondeat superior*.

The are only two basic types of authority. The agent can have actual authority or the agent can have apparent authority. The testable situation within actual authority is implied authority. The candidate should be prepared for an implied-actual authority question. An agent's implied authority is the type of authority an agent has in order to carry out his/her expressed-actual authority. Implied authority flows from necessity and custom.

More likely the CPA will test on apparent authority. Apparent authority is the type of authority created by the principal. Here the principal has done (or has not done) something to lead a third party to believe that the agent has the authority. An apparent authority question would be tested in a situation where the agent has exceeded his/her actual authority or where the principal has terminated the agent's actual authority and the agent is still performing.

Remember, there is nothing the agent can do to create apparent authority. Tell the testers this and receive extra points. The AICPA has tested on this principle by having the principal and the agent agree to an indemnification agreement. Here the agent agrees, in contract, to indemnify the principal for his/her poor performance. This agreement has no effect on the third party. First tell the examiners that the third party is not in privity of contract with either parties. Also, the indemnification does not limit the third party unless the third party is aware of the agreement.

In addition, the agent owes his/her principal a duty of loyalty. The candidate should study all duties owed by both parties. If the agent breaches his/her duty of loyalty, the principal may ask for damages or for a constructive trust. Another duty owed by the agent to his/her principal is the duty of notification. Anything the agent knows, the principal knows. This is called imputed knowledge. The principal can sue the agent for breach of this duty.

The agent can bind the principal in contract, tort or crime. The AICPA has tested on tort, but contract liability is fairly complicated and criminal liability is undergoing development. These issues would make good essay questions.

The agent binds his/her principal in tort under the doctrine of *respondeat superior*. The principal "responds" for the tortious acts of their employees, if the employee commits the tort within the scope of the agent/employee's duties (job description). In this case the employer is strictly liable for the tortious acts of the employee.

The most likely scenario is negligence. If the agent commits a negligent act within the scope of his/her employment, then the employer is strictly liable. For example, a pizza parlor hires a student to drive its delivery truck. The student, during a pizza delivery, accidently runs over an elderly lady. Who is liable and why?

Remember, the employee is liable for his/her own torts. But the examiners will want to know about the employer's liability. Here, the employer would be liable since the tort (negligence) was committed within the scope (driving a delivery truck) of the agent/employee's employment. The examiners will probably not test on intentional torts. Very few jobs have job descriptions that include an intentional tort. A few exceptions are bar bouncers, policemen, and bodyguards.

NOVEMBER, 1995 NUMBER 2a
INDEPENDENT CONTRACTOR

Issues Tested:

      I.   Written Agency Contracts
      II.   Implied and Express Authority
      III. Termination of Agency and Notification
      IV. Principal Liability in Contract
      V.   Disclosed Principal Liability in Contract

REGULATION OF EMPLOYMENT

This section is growing in testing importance. You should be aware of the latest law concerning rates and limits of the different Federal Employment Laws. All questions listed are original questions.

I. Social Security (FICA)

Social Security and FICA are the popular areas in the Regulation of Employment section.

   A. General Purpose\Coverage

      1. Employers must file quarterly and can ask for reimbursement from the employee. (WT)

      2. If the employer does not withhold FICA from the employee nor supply taxpayer identification numbers, the employer can be held primarily liable for the employee's portion and other penalties. (WTTT)

May 1985 #31

Which of the following statements is correct regarding social security taxes?

   a. The annual contributions made by a self-employed person with net earnings of $30,000 in 1985 will be the same as the combined contributions made by an employee and employer on that same amount.
   b. A self-employed person is subject to social security taxes based on that person's gross earnings from self-employment.
   c. **An employer who fails to withhold and pay the employee's portion of social security taxes remains primarily liable for the employee's share.**
   d. An individual who receives net earnings from self-employment of $30,000 and wages of $30,000 in 1985 will be subject to social security taxes on $60,000.

CHAPTER 35   SECTION 4   PAGES 630-631

3. Wages include cash and other media of payment, but wages do not include individual interest, dividends or other gains. (WT)

4. Social security benefits coverage includes divorced spouses, disabled children and medicare recipients (do not confuse with medicaid) (T)

5. Payments to children end when the child reaches the age of 18 or when the child is no longer a full-time high school student, whichever is later (3 months after the student becomes 19). (WT)

B. Payments

1. The candidate should know the tax percentages of the self employed and FICA employees. (WT)

2. Employers do receive a credit for state taxes paid. (T)

3. Social Security benefits can be taxed, but there are limits. (WTT)

4. Receipt of payments under private pensions do not limit social security payments. (T)

5. FICA payments are deductible as a business expense. (WTTT)

6. Director fees have been taxable. (T)

II. Employee Safety (Worker's Compensation)

A. General Purpose

1. Worker's Compensation is a state system for providing a convenient forum where employees can apply and receive compensation for work-related injuries, diseases and aggravation of pre-existing diseases. (TTT)

2. There is no Worker's Compensation for intentionally self-inflicted injuries. (T)

3. Worker's Compensation does not provide for the full payment of benefits, but provides a percentage of the cost. (T)

4. Worker's Compensation laws are liberally construed for the employee. (T)

5. Worker's Compensation payments to insurance companies are not deducted

from an employee's salary. The payments are made by the employer. (WT)

B. Standard of Proof

   1. With Worker's Compensation, a worker is barred from the common-law right to sue his/her employer for the work-related injury. However, the employer cannot use any common-law defenses. These common-law defenses include assumption of the risk, contributory or comparative negligence, or the fellow servant rule. In essence, Worker's Compensation is comparable to strict liability. The employee does not have to prove negligence on the part of his/her employer. (TTT)

November 1993 # 36

Which one of the following statements concerning Worker's Compensation laws is generally correct?

   a. Employers are strictly liable without regard to whether or not they are at fault.
   b. Worker's Compensation benefits are not available if the employee is negligent.
   c. Worker's Compensation awards are not reviewable by courts.
   d. The amount of damages recoverable is based on comparative negligence.

CHAPTER 35   SECTION 3   PAGE 630

C. Coverage

   1. Not all workers are covered. Certain domestic, transitory and agriculture workers are not covered. In addition, each state requires a certain minimal number of eligible employees before state law applies. (T)

   2. Worker's Compensation is not always the exclusive remedy for the injured worker. If the injuries are the result of a product liability claim or an intentional tort claim against the employer, the employee may also file his/her own separate law suit. (TT)

May 1981 # 60

Musgrove Manufacturing Enterprises is subject to compulsory Worker's

> Compensation laws in the state in which it does business. It has complied with the state's Worker's Compensation provisions. State law provides that where there has been compliance, Worker's Compensation is normally an exclusive remedy. However, the remedy will not be exclusive if the
>
>   **a. employee has been intentionally injured by the employer personally.**
>   b. employee dies as a result of his/her injuries.
>   c. accident was entirely the fault of a fellow servant of the employee.
>   d. employer was only slightly negligent and the employee's conduct was grossly negligent.
>
> CHAPTER 35   SECTION 4   PAGE 630

    3.   If an independent contractor is injured on the job, he/she can sue the person responsible for the tort (e.g. the employee). This plaintiff can, also, sue the employer under the *respondeat superior* doctrine. (TT)

III. Employment Discrimination

This is a relatively new section for the CPA Exam. Like other new and infrequently tested areas, the AICPA does not test in depth. However, the candidate should expect more in depth questions in time. For instance, Sexual Harassment and Quid Pro Quo are prime areas for future testing.

    A.   Protected classes under Title VII (of the Civil Rights Act of 1964 as amended in 1991)

    Title VII covers employment discrimination in the areas of race, color, sex, religion, and national origin. (T) But Title VII does <u>not</u> cover age. ADEA covers age discrimination in employment.

    B.   BFOQ (Bona Fide Occupational Qualification)

    As discussed above, there are several protected groups. However, there are times when an employer can claim that the particular job cannot be filled by someone in a protected class. This is called a BFOQ defense. For instance, a rabbi could not be a priest or vice versa. It is a bona fide occupational qualification that a priest should be a Catholic. Therefore, the rabbi could not assert that he was discriminated against because of his/her religion. However, the AICPA will expect the candidate to know that race can <u>never</u> be a BFOQ! (T)

Regulation of Employment 121

    C.   The Equal Employment Opportunity Commission (EEOC) can file a law suit on behalf of the employee. (T)

    D.   The Federal Age Discrimination in Employment Act (ADEA) prohibits employment discrimination for applicants and employees 40 years of age or older. The act specifically prohibits compulsory retirement for employees under 65, but not for termination for cause. (T) ADEA provides for back pay, but not early retirement. (T)

IV.   Fair Labor Standards Act (FLSA) (Minimum Wage and Overtime) (T)

    A.   Agency powers include subpoena, wage orders, and investigative powers. (WT)

    B.   Coverage

        1.   Some workers are covered under minimum wage, but not covered for overtime. (WT)

        2.   There are several groups excluded from the act or from portions of the act (e.g. students, children, agriculture workers). (WT)

        3.   The FLSA applies to hourly, weekly, and monthly bases of pay. (T)

        4.   An employee is entitled to overtime if they work more than 40 hours in a week. (T)

V.   Occupational Safety and Health Act (OSHA)

        1.   An employer cannot fire an employee for reporting OSHA violations. (T)

        2.   OSHA can use "on-site" inspection based on a employee's request. (T)

VI.   The Consolidated Omnibus Budget Reconciliation Act of 1985 (COBRA)

An employee who voluntarily resigns can still receive medical insurance coverage for 18 months ('94). (T)

VII.   FUTA (unemployment) joint Federal/State Administration

    A.   Allows for employer to take a credit for state contributions. (WTT)

B. Deductible as a business expense. (WTT)

> November 1984 #37
>
> Federal unemployment taxes
>
> a. are deductible by an employee on his/her individual tax return.
> b. **are deductible as a business expense on the federal income tax return of a corporate employer.**
> c. may be offset by a credit equal to the amount of the federal tax liability if the employer contributes to an approved state unemployment fund.
> d. are imposed on the employer and employee.
>
> CHAPTER N/A   SECTION N/A   PAGE N/A (but see page 631)

C. Employers, not employees, pay into the fund. (T)

D. Covers employees discharged due to no fault of their (employee's) own. Applicants are not eligible if they are discharged for cause. (T)

E. The tax is a percentage of the employee's salary to the statutory limit. (T)

VIII. Americans With Disabilities Act of 1990

A. The Act protects disabled persons from discrimination in public transportation and privately operated public accommodations. (T)

IX. Employee Retirement Income Security Act of 1974 (ERISA)

A. In a noncontributory retirement plan, all funds are provided by the employer. (WT)

B. Under ERISA an employer is prevented from delaying an employee's participation in the pension. (WT)

C. ERISA regulates employee vesting rules and plan funding. (T)

X. Equal Pay Act

A. Just as with Title VII, the Equal Pay Act prohibits discrimination based upon sex. (T)

XI. National Labor Relations Act (The Wagner Act)

    A. Sick pay and vacation pay are not exempt from the Act. (T)

ESSAY QUESTION

    The only essay question from this section tests on Worker's Compensation. However, there are other testable areas. Since the CPA Exam tests rather heavily on social security law, the candidate would expect a question from this section. Yet, social security is straightforward. For example, multiple choice questions are the proper venue for testing the types of benefits, tax rates and the deductibility. There is very little room for discussion, However, the AICPA could create a essay question that focuses on one particular employee and his/her eligibility and cost for certain benefits.

Another potential area of testing is ERISA. Pensions law is a growing area of concern. ERISA is complex to administer, but the basics of pension law would be testable.

Just within the last few years, the AICPA began testing in the area of employment discrimination. This is an excellent area of testing. Students should be prepared for testing concerning the *prima facie* cases of disparate treatment and disparate\adverse impact under Title VII. The candidate should be familiar with the defenses of business necessity, job relatedness and BFOQ. This area could reach into age discrimination and the Americans with Disabilities Act. If the AICPA is testing on environmental law, then the expansion of modern employment law is next.

NOVEMBER, 1988 NUMBER 3
WORKER'S COMPENSATION

Issues Tested:

    I. Eligibility
    II. Standards of Proof
    III. Exclusive Remedy

Worker's Compensation is the employee remedy for injuries suffered from work-related accidents. Therefore, the injury must be accidental, not intentionally self inflicted. While an employee cannot directly sue the employer for the negligence of another employee, Worker's Compensation does not cover intentional torts of fellow employees.

Also, AICPA can also test on the difference between an employee who is covered by Worker's Compensation and the independent contractor who is not covered by the statute. The candidate should be familiar with all the factors that the law uses to determine independent contractor status. The factors include the degree of control, skill required, method of payment and the party who supplied the tools. The candidate should be aware that no one factor is significant, but this evaluation is a totality of the factors test.

Finally, the candidate should address the exclusive remedy issue. Generally, Worker's Compensation is the sole remedy for work related accidents. The employer is without its common-law defenses. These common-law defenses include contributory or comparative negligence, assumption of the risk and the fellow servant rule. Worker's Compensation is strict liability for the employer.

But for removing the common-law defenses of the employer and the relative ease for recovery of injuries, the employee cannot also sue his/her employer. Yet, there are two known situations where Worker's Compensation is not the exclusive remedy for the employee. The first exception is product liability. If the employee can show that an improperly designed or manufactured machine injured him/her, the employee could recover from Worker's Compensation and, also, sue the manufacturer of the defective machine. Also, if the employer intentionally injured the employee, the employee could also sue his/her employer.

GENERAL PARTNERSHIPS (PARTNERSHIPS)

I. Definition

    A. The partnership definition is deceptively simple. A partnership is an association of two or more persons who manage a business together and share profits. (TTT) This definition is similar for the IRS, the state's common-law definition and the state's statutory definition under the Uniform Partnership Act (Part II, Sec. 6(1) of the UPA). In fact, the definition of "persons" under the UPA includes individuals, corporations and other partnerships (Part I, Sec. 2). The courts look to the intent of the parties. However, courts do not look to the intent to be a partnership, but to the intent to do the enumerate acts under Section 6(1). Therefore, you might never intend to become a partnership, but if you intend to manage a business with another and share profits, then you are a partnership. Also, partnership law and agency law are very similar.

May 1982 #1

Three independent sole proprietors decided to pool their resources and form a partnership. The business assets and liabilities of each were transferred to the partnership. The partnership commenced business on September 1, 1981, but the parties did not execute a formal partnership agreement until October 15, 1981. Which of the following is correct?

    a. The existing creditors must consent to the transfer of the individual business assets to the partnership.
    b. The partnership began its existence on September 1, 1981.
    c. If the partnership's duration is indefinite, the partnership agreement must be in writing and signed.

> d. In the absence of a partnership agreement specifically covering division of losses among the partners, they will be deemed to share them in accordance with their capital contributions.
>
> CHAPTER 38   SECTION 1   PAGES 683-684

B. Joint Venture

A JOINT VENTURE is not a partnership. A joint venture meets part of the definition in Section 6 (1), but there is no "managing" a business. The joint venture is for one transaction or a limited number of transactions. (TT)

The joint venture may be treated as a partnership for tax purposes. Yet, it will not be treated as a partnership for liability purposes (see tort, contract and agency law).

> November 1989 #4
>
> A joint venture is a (an)
>
> a. association limited to no more than two persons in business for profit.
> b. enterprise of numerous co-owners in a nonprofit undertaking.
> c. corporate enterprise for a single undertaking of limited duration.
> **d. association of persons engaged as co-owners in a single undertaking for profit.**
>
> CHAPTER 37   SECTION 8   PAGE 674

II. Nature of Partnerships

A. Entity Approach

A partnership is considered to be a distinct ENTITY for certain legal purposes which include:

1. FICA and FUTA deductions (T)

2. Worker's Compensation (T)

3. They can sue and be sued in the legal system. (T)

4. Owning property in the partnerships name. (T)

B. Aggregate Approach

1. For tax purposes, the partnership is held to be an aggregate of separate tax paying partners. There is no separate Partnership Tax. (TT)

III. Formation

A. Fictitious Name Statute.

Under state law, a partnership cannot use a name that is used by another business entity. Although a violation of this statute will not directly effect the status of the formation, there could be a fine for the violation. (TT) This is not the same as trademark law. The AICPA does not test on Intellectual Property Law in the Law section.

November 1983 # 15

Many states require partnerships to file the partnership name under laws which are generally known as fictitious name statutes. These statutes

   a. require a proper filing as a condition precedent to the valid creation of a partnership.
   b. are designed primarily to provide registration for tax purposes.
   c. are designed to clarify the rights and duties of the members of the partnership.
   d. **have little effect on the creation or operation of a partnership other than the imposition of a fine for noncompliance.**

CHAPTER N/A   SECTION N/A   PAGE N/A

B. Implied

A partnership can be formed by implication. (T) See the above discussion concerning UPA Section 6(1).

C. Expressed

In this situation the partners have either expressed orally their wishes to be in partnership or have expressed so in writing. (T)

1. Writing

    The issue in the CPA Exam is <u>when must</u> the partnership agreement be in writing. The agreement must conform with the state's Statute of Frauds rule. This rule states that if the underlying transaction requires a writing under the state's Statute of Frauds, then the partnership agreement must also be in writing. Examples include:

    a. Land (T)

    b. One Year (T)

2. Contents

    It is recommended that the partners agree on the share of ownership, profits and losses, partner relationships and dissolution. (T)

IV. Rights of a Partner

Generally, each partner must be treated equally. As the UPA states, each partner has one vote. Majority controls in ordinary matters, while a unanimous vote is required for major matters. While the AICPA does not test on these concepts specifically, the candidate should understand them.

A. Transfer of Partnership Interest

1. A partner has the right to transfer (or pledge) his/her interest (profits and surplus) in the partnership. (TTT)

May 1983 #4

Donovan, a partner of Monroe, Lincoln, and Washington, is considering selling or pledging all or part of his interest in the partnership. The partnership agreement is silent on the matter. Donovan can

a. sell part but not all of his partnership interest.
b. sell or pledge his entire partnership interest without causing a dissolution.

> c. pledge his/her partnership interest, but only with the consent of his fellow partners.
> d. sell his entire partnership interest and confer partner status upon the purchaser.
>
> CHAPTER 39   SECTION 1   PAGE 701

2. This transfer will not cause dissolution. (TT)

3. While an assignee of the partnership has no right to become a partner (no partner can have another thrust upon him/her), the assignee is entitled to his/her assignor's share of the partnership profits. (TT)

B. Partnership Profits and Property

1. A partner has a right to partnership profits. The AICPA, however, will test on the allocation of profits and losses, absent an agreement. The UPA states that absent this allocation agreement (e.g. silence) profits are to be divided equally. (T) Losses always follow profits, again if the loss allocation is silent. (TT)

2. Partners have no legal interest in partnership property.

   a. Partners are considered to be tenants in partnership. (T) A partner who contributed the property is still a tenant in partnership.

   b. The partner can assign his/her partnership interest, but he/she cannot assign partnership property. (T)

C. Management

One would expect the AICPA to test in this area. However, this area receives little attention.

1. Partners are not, because of their status as a partner, employees. (T) Partners are expected to work full time for the partnership and without remuneration. However, a partner can become an employee.

V. Liability

A. Contract Liability

1. A partner has joint liability in contract. (TTT)

2. A partner can bind the other partners in contract. (T) See Authority.

B. Tort Liability

1. A partner has joint and several liability in tort. (TTT)

2. A partner can impose tort liability on the other partners. (T) The tort must be committed within the scope of his/her partnership duties. (See *respondeat superior* in Agency.)

C. Limitation of Liability

1. A partner, in a partnership, has unlimited liability. (TTT)

2. If the partnership agreement has a "hold harmless" clause, this clause is binding on the partners, but it is not binding on non-partners who did not sign (e.g. creditors of all kinds). (TTT)

D. Incoming Liability

1. An incoming or newly admitted partner is liable for the debts and obligations of the partnership prior to his/her admittance. However, he/she is only liable to the extent of his/her capital contribution. (TTT) From admittance on, the new partner will have unlimited liability. Admittance does not require the contribution of property or services, but a vote of the other partners. (T)

E. Marshalling

1. Under the old common-law concept known as marshalling, a creditor of the partnership must first exhaust partnership assets before the creditor can execute on the individual partner's assets. (T)

VI. Authority

A. Implied Authority

1. A partner has IMPLIED AUTHORITY to bind the partnership in contract. (TT)

General Partnerships   131

November 1991 # 15

In a general partnership, the authorization of all partners is required for an individual partner to bind the partnership in a business transaction to

    a.   purchase inventory.
    b.   hire employees.
    c.   sell goodwill.
    d.   sign advertising contracts.

CHAPTER 38   SECTION 4   PAGE 695-696

---

2. For liability, as well as rights and duties, partners are principals and agents of the other partners. (T) See Agency.

3. There are certain actions that partners have <u>no</u> implied authority to bind.

    a.   Confession of Judgment (T)

    b.   Assignment for the Benefit of the Creditors (T)

    c.   Surety (T)

    d.   Arbitration (TT)

    e.   Accommodation (T)

    f.   Dispose Goodwill (T)

B. Apparent Authority

1. Any APPARENT AUTHORITY limitations must be known to the third parties. If the third party has knowledge of this limitation imposed by the partner(s), then there is no liability. (TTT)

November 1993 # 12

The apparent authority of a partner to bind the partnership in dealing with third parties

132 Business Law and the CPA Exam

> a. **will be effectively limited by a formal resolution of the partners of which third parties are aware.**
> b. will be effectively limited by a formal resolution of the partners of which third parties are unaware.
> c. would permit a partner to submit a claim against the partnership to arbitration.
> d. must be derived from the express powers and purposes contained in the partnership agreement.
>
> CHAPTER 38   SECTION 4   PAGE 695

II. Termination (Dissolution and Winding Up)

　A. Dissolution

　Again the AICPA does not test much on DISSOLUTION (although it is listed on their outline). The AICPA tests more or the Winding Up process. In any event, partnerships do not unlimited duration. (T)

　　1. If the Partnership is silent as to the duration of the partnership, then the partnership is terminable at the will of any partner. (T)

　B. Winding Up

　The candidate should be prepared to do a math problem on partnership WINDING UP in either the multiple choice section or in the essay section.

　　1. Normally during winding up, the partners choose a partner to wind up the business of the partnership. The authority to carry on business terminates, but this partner does have the authority to wind up. (T)

　　2. Distribution order under the UPA for a solvent partnership (T)

　　　a. Outside creditors who are <u>not</u> partners.

　　　b. Partners who have made advances (e.g. loans).

　　　c. Partners' capital contribution.

　　　d. Partners' share of the profits or surplus.

3. There is a specific situation that adds a twist to the above scenario. If a partner must pay more than his/her share of partnership debt, this partner may demand contribution from the other partners. (T)

May 1988 # 13

X, Y, and Z have capital balances of $30,000, $15,000 and $5,000, respectively, in the XYZ Partnership. The general partnership agreement is silent as to the manner in which partnership losses are to be allocated, but does provide that partnership profits are to be allocated as follows: 40% to X, 25% to Y, and 35% to Z. The partners have decided to dissolve and liquidate the partnership. After paying all creditors, the amount available for distribution will be $20,000. X, Y and Z are individually solvent. Under the circumstance, Z will

- a. receive $7,000.
- b. receive $12,000.
- **c. personally have to contribute an additional $5,500.**
- d. personally have to contribute an additional $5,000.

ANSWER: C

Solution: Since this is a solvent partnership, (the creditors have been paid) the candidate should first calculate the loss as follows:

	Partnership	X	Y	Z
Capital Accounts:	$50,000 =	$30,000	$15,000	$5,000
Loss Allocation: (If the partnership agreement is silent, then losses follow profits.)		40%	25%	35%
Loss:	($30,000)	($12,000)	($7,500)	($10,500)
Final Accounts:	$20,000	$18,000	$7,500	($5,500)

Therefore, while Z contributed smaller amounts to the partnership, his profit/loss allocation will require him to pay in additional amounts at winding up.

CHAPTER N/A   SECTION N/A   PAGE N/A (but see pages 703-705)

ESSAY QUESTIONS

The CPA Exam tests infrequently on Partnerships in the essay questions. The questions do not cover new material beyond those issues tested in the multiple choice questions. If you can remember the multiple choice questions, plus the rules of Agency law, you should be prepared for partnership essays.

NOVEMBER, 1988 NUMBER 4
LIABILITY AND AUTHORITY

Issues Tested:

  I.   Authority
  II. Liability
  III. Notice
  IV. Marshalling

First, in order to hold the partners and the partnership liable, the candidate must discuss liability. Just as with the multiple choice questions, the AICPA tests on apparent authority. Apparent authority cannot be created by the agent, but by the actions of the principal.

Next, the candidate must show how liability should be allocated. A favorite topic is the liability of the incoming partner. Here, the incoming partner <u>does</u> have personal liability for actions taken before his/her admittance. But, he/she will only be liable to the extent of his/her capital contribution. But, after admission the new partner has unlimited liability. This liability is joint in contract and joint and several in tort.

Notice is an issue with liability. The withdrawing partner can avoid liability with proper notice. The withdrawing partner must give actual notice to his/her partners and to third parties who have dealt with that partner personally. Everyone else is only entitled to constructive or published notice.

MAY, 1991 NUMBER 2
DUTIES AND LIABILITY

Issues Tested:

  I. Duties
  II. Liability
  IV. Indemnity Agreements

Partners are principals and agents of the other partners. Therefore, it is very easy for liability and duties to attach. Partners must abide by the limitations in the partnership agreements, but third parties are not bound by such agreements.

Partners can bind the other partner in contract and in tort. The contract rules are difficult, but no one is liable in contract unless his/her name appears (see Article 3 of the UCC). Partners owe the other partners fiduciary duties. The law is vigilant to protect fiduciary duties, and the CPA Exam will test on this protection.

Incoming partners have unique liability problems. These new partners are liable for debts prior to admission, but only to the extent of their capital contribution. However, the AICPA tests frequently on indemnity agreements. For instance, if the partners agree to indemnify partners from third party lawsuit damages, the third party is not bound by this agreement. The third party can proceed directly against that partner and ignore the indemnity agreement. The third party is not a party to this contract.

LONG OBJECTIVE QUESTIONS
May, 1995 NUMBER 2a

Issues Tested:

I. Statute of Frauds
II. The UPA definition of a partnership (see IA)
III. The sharing of partnership profits
IV. The sharing of partnership losses
V. Termination of a partnership and notice requirements
VI. Partner tort liability

LIMITED PARTNERSHIPS

Because of the passing of the Tax Reform Act of 1986, Limited Partnerships have not remained a favorite choice as a business formation. However, with a change in the tax code and the emergence of the Family Limited Partnership, as an estate planning tool, Limited Partnerships could still be significant. The AICPA still tests on the subject, yet not in the same depth as Corporations and Partnerships. The candidate should be aware of the statutory law that governs Limited Partnerships. The newest uniform law adopted by most states is the Revised Uniform Limited Partnership Act (RULPA).

I. Nature and Formation

    A. Limited partnerships, just like corporations, require a state statute. (TT)

May 1985 #7

Which of the following statements is correct regarding a limited partnership?

    a. The general partner must make a capital contribution.
    b. **It can only be created pursuant to a statute providing for the formation of limited partnerships.**
    c. It can be created with limited liability for all partners.
    d. At least one general partner must also be a limited partner.

CHAPTER 39   SECTION 2   PAGE 705

    B. One General Partner and one Limited Partner are required. (T)

II. Rights of the Partners

    A. General Partners

        1. A general partner may be a secured creditor. (T)

2. A general partner may be a limited partner at the same time. (WTT)

3. The general partner may assign his/her interest. (WTT)

November 1983 # 18

Vast Ventures is a limited partnership. The partnership agreement does not contain provisions dealing with the assignment of a partnership interest. The rights of the general and limited partners regarding the assignment of their partnership interests are

   a. determined according to the common law of partnerships as articulated by the courts.
   b. basically the same with respect to both types of partners.
   c. basically the same with the exception that the limited partner must give ten days notice prior to the assignment.
   d. different in that the assignee of the general partnership interest does not become a substituted partner, whereas the assignee of a limited partnership interest automatically becomes a substituted limited partner.

CHAPTER N/A   SECTION N/A   PAGE N/A

B. Limited Partners

   1. Limited partners have inspection rights which could include the right to inspect the tax records. (T)

   2. Limited partners may assign their interests.

      a. An assignee of the limited partnership interest has the right to receive his/her portion of limited partnership's profits and the return of his/her contribution. In order to have all the remaining rights (inspection, accounting etc.), the assignee must become a SUBSTITUTE limited partner. Here, all partners must vote for the inclusion, and the limited partnership certificate must be changed. (WTTT)

May 1987 # 8

White, Grey, and Fox formed a limited partnership. White is the general partner and Grey and Fox are the limited partners. Each agreed to contribute $200,000. Grey and Fox each contributed $200,000 in cash while White contributed $150,000 in cash and $50,000 worth of services already rendered. After two years, the partnership is insolvent. The fair market value of the assets of the partnership is $150,000, and the liabilities total $275,000. The partners have made no withdrawals.

Unless otherwise provided in the certificate of limited partnership, which of the following is correct if Grey dies?

    a.   Grey's executor will automatically become a substituted limited partner.
    b.   **Grey's executor will have all the rights of a limited partner for the purpose of settling the estate.**
    c.   The partnership will automatically be dissolved.
    d.   Grey's estate will be free from any liabilities which may have been incurred by Grey as a limited partner.

CHAPTER N/A   SECTION N/A   PAGE N/A

May 1987 #9

Unless otherwise provided in the certificate of limited partnership, which of the following is correct if Fox assigns her interest in the partnership to Barr and only White consents to Barr's admission as a limited partner?

    a.   **Barr will not become a substituted limited partner unless Grey also consents.**
    b.   Barr will have the right to inspect the partnership's books.
    c.   The partnership will be dissolved.
    d.   Barr will become a substituted limited partner because White, as general partner, consented.

CHAPTER N/A   SECTION N/A   PAGE N/A

---

    b.   An executor of an estate may be a limited partner in order to settle the estate, but he/she is not automatically a substitute limited partner; they must be elected. (WT)

140   Business Law and the CPA Exam

III. Liabilities of the Partners

   A. General Partners

   General partners have unlimited liability. However, the AICPA seems not to be testing in this area. The AICPA will test this concept under General Partnerships. But the candidate will be tested on limited partners' liability.

   B. Limited Partners

      1. Limited partners have limited liability up to the amounts of contribution.

      2. However, a limited partner can be treated as a general partner for liability purposes (unlimited), if the limited partner does any of the following:

         a. Manages the business. (TT)

May 1982 #3

Stanley is a well-known retired movie personality who purchased a limited partnership interest in Terrific Movie Productions upon its initial syndication. Terrific has three general partners, who also purchased limited partnership interests, and 1,000 additional limited partners located throughout the United States. Which of the following is correct?

   a. If Stanley permits his name to be used in connection with the business and is held out as a participant in the management of the venture, he will be liable as a general partner.
   b. The sale of these limited partnership interests would not be subject to SEC registration.
   c. This limited partnership may be created with the same informality as a general partnership.
   d. The general partners are prohibited from also owning limited partnership interests.

CHAPTER 39   SECTION 2   PAGES 706-707

---

         b. Lends his/her name to the business. (TT)

         c. Knows about defective formation, but fails to withdraw.

3. Limited partners have the right to an accounting. (T)

IV. Dissolution and Distribution

A. Dissolution

The AICPA does not test in this area. However, the candidate should be aware the focus of a potential dissolution question would be the general partner.

B. Distribution

This could be a area of confusion. The AICPA tests in this area and expects the candidate to know that the general partner is the last to be paid under the old Uniform Limited Partnership Act (ULPA). However, in the more modern and the more widely used RULPA, the general partners and the limited partners are treated equally. In other words, at distribution the RULPA treats a limited partnership as a general partnership. (T)

ESSAY QUESTION

NOVEMBER, 1986 NUMBER 2
GENERAL PARTNER AND LIMITED PARTNER

Issues Tested:

I. Definitions
II. Liability
III. Transfer of Interest
IV. Buy/Sell Agreements

By definition a limited partnership requires one general partner and one limited partner. The general partner manages the business, while the limited partner is a passive investor.

The general partner has unlimited liability for limited partnership debts. The limited partner enjoys limited liability protection. The limited partner can, for liability purposes only, become a general partner if the limited partner: 1) lends his/her name to the business, 2) manages the business, 3) or knows of defective formation and fails to withdraw.

The limited partner has the right to transfer his/her interest. The transferee can become a substituted limited partner if all the members, except the assignor, consent. The general partner can also transfer his/her partnership interest. All partners must admit the assignee as the new general partner.

The death of the general partner dissolves the limited partnership. In order to keep the limited partnership from terminating, the partners can agree in advance to a buy/sell agreement. Therefore, the partnership can continue. The same instrument is used to prevent a general partnership from terminating.

Corporations

Ironically, the AICPA does not test heavily in the Corporation section. Since the use of the corporate form is extremely popular, the candidate would expect a heavy concentration in this area. In addition, Business Law texts follow this approach. However, while the number of questions asked by the AICPA is not in proportion to amount of law studied, the questions cover a wide area. Therefore, you should be prepared for any type of question.

I. Nature Formation and Operation

Corporations are legal but artificial "Persons." The corporation has perpetual existence (T). The AICPA follows the Revised Model Business Code (RMBCA). There is no present indication that the AICPA will test on the new hybrid forms of the standard corporate forms. These hybrids include close corporations and limited liability companies. You should be prepared to be tested on these despite the AICPA's silence.

   A. State (statute) Creation

   Corporations, like limited partnerships, are creations of state law. (TTT) One must receive approval from a state official in order to do business in the corporate form.

May 1985 # 11

Which of the following is a correct statement concerning the similarities of a limited partnership and corporation?

   a.   Both are recognized for federal income tax purposes as taxable entities.
   b.   **Both can only be created pursuant to a statute and each must file a copy of its certificate with the proper state authorities.**
   c.   Both provide insulation from personal liability for all of the owners of the business.

144 Business Law and the CPA Exam

> d. Shareholders and limited partners may both participate in the management of the business and retain limited liability.
>
> CHAPTER 40   SECTION 1   PAGES 713-714

B. Articles of Incorporation

While a candidate does not have to know his/her individual state's incorporation requirements, he/she should be generally familiar with the requirements of standard ARTICLES OF INCORPORATION. Testable elements or steps include:

1. Name of the corporation (TT)

2. Number of shares authorized (TTT)

3. Corporation's registered agent (TT)

4. The articles do not include the names of the officers, nor the quorum requirements. (T)

> May 1984 #10
>
> Generally, articles of incorporation must contain all of the following except the
>
> a. names of the incorporators.
> b. name of the corporation.
> c. number of shares authorized.
> **d. names of initial officers and their terms of office.**
>
> CHAPTER 40   SECTION 4   PAGES 722-724

C. Initial Capital Structure

1. Watered Stock

    A shareholder can not receive valuable company stock for worthless assets. (T)

2. There can be no issuance of shares for future services (T)

3. Newly issued shares must be issued at par or above par. (T)

4. The organizational expenses can be paid from the stock subscriptions. (T)

D. Annual Meetings

Annual meetings confirm Board actions. (T)

II. Classification of Corporations

A. Foreign Corporation

A FOREIGN CORPORATION is not a corporation from another country. A foreign corporation is a corporation formed in one state, but doing business in another state. The foreign corporation must receive a license or certificate to do business in the other (forum) state. (T)

B. Sub S Corporation

The SUB S CORPORATION enjoys multiple benefits. First, it has the corporate shield, but it is taxed as a partnership. The CPA candidate should be familiar with the following requirements:

1. Sub S must be a domestic corporation.

2. The corporation must not be a member of an affiliated group of corporations.

3. The corporation must have 35 or fewer shareholders. (T)

4. These shareholders can only be individuals, estates and certain trusts.

5. The corporation can have only one class of stock. (T)

6. There can be no shareholder who is a nonresident alien.

III. Capital Structure

The AICPA will also tests on the equity side of the balance sheet during the Business Law section. Few Business Law texts provide all the information needed for this area. Please refer back to your accounting texts for further assistance.

146 Business Law and the CPA Exam

- A. Treasury Stock/Shares

    1. Treasury shares are not canceled shares. (WT)

    2. Treasury stock may be used for a stock dividend. (WT)

    3. Treasury stock may be sold for less than par value. (WTT)

- B. Dividends

    1. Stock dividends decrease retained earnings. (WT)

    2. Dividends have no effect (deductibility) on federal taxes. (WTT)

    3. With the declaration of a cumulative preferred stock dividend, the preferred stockholder becomes an unsecured creditor. (TT)

    4. Accumulated Earnings Tax

        The IRS will try to force a dividend by placing a high tax for hording undistributed earnings. (WT) The hording of dividends is permissible for providing enough cash flow during the operation cycle (the *Bardahl* case) and for legitimate expansion needs (the *Faber* case).

    5. Cash, property and liquidating dividends are asset or capital distributions. A stock split is not a capital distribution. (T)

- C. Debt

    1. Convertible bonds are debt securities.

IV. Duties (Fiduciary), Liabilities and Rights

- A. Promoter Liability

    Prior to incorporation, a promoter is liable on the contracts he/she signs.

    1. If the corporation is not formed, the promoter remains liable. (T)

    2. The promoter remains liable on the preincorporation contract unless the contract states the promoter is not liable or there is a novation. A novation substitutes the corporation for the promoter. The corporation is not liable until there is a

ratification (expressed or implied). (T)

3. The promoter owes the corporation fiduciary duties. (T)

B. Directors, Officers and Majority Shareholder Duties

1. Officers are agents of the corporations, who have actual and apparent authority to act. In addition, they owe the corporation fiduciary duties (T)

2. Directors, officers and even majority shareholders owe the corporation fiduciary duties. (T) There is no significant case law that places fiduciary duties on minority shareholders.

3. The officers and directors of a corporation owe the corporation the fiduciary duty of loyalty. Loyalty would include no undisclosed conflicts of interest and no competition with the corporation. However, with full disclosure, the director or officer could participate. (T)

C. Liability of Directors and Officers

1. For violating a fiduciary duty, a corporation can demand a return of the money or property (T). This return would be a constructive trust, which is more of a remedy than a legal trust.

   a) An *ultra vires* act by the directors or officers is a breach of this fiduciary duty. (T)

2. The directors and officers have a powerful defense to a derivative suit. The "Business Judgement Rule" will insulate corporate officers and directors for good faith errors in judgment. (T)

November 1985 #3

Jane Cox, a shareholder of Mix Corp., has properly commenced a derivative action against Mix's Board of Directors. Cox alleges that the Board breached its fiduciary duty and was negligent by failing to independently verify the financial statements prepared by management upon which Smart & Co., CPAs, issued an unqualified opinion. The financial statements contained inaccurate information which the Board relied upon in committing large sums of money to capital expansion. This resulted in Mix having to borrow money at extremely high interest rates to meet current cash needs. Within a short period of time, the price of Mix Corp. stock declined drastically. Which of the following statements is correct?

- a. The Board is strictly liable, regardless of fault, since it owes a fiduciary duty to both the corporation and the shareholders.
- b. The Board is liable since any negligence of Smart is automatically imputed to the Board.
- **c. The Board may avoid liability if it acted in good faith and in a reasonable manner.**
- d. The Board may avoid liability in all cases where it can show that it lacked scienter.

CHAPTER 41   SECTION 4   PAGES 738-739

D. Rights of Directors and Officers

1. Indemnification

    Officers and directors who win or lose a derivative suit can ask for payment from the corporation for cost, fees, etc. This payment can be made even if the director or officer is negligent. (TT)

2. The director has a right to inspect corporate records and has a right to rely on the information. (T)

3. The directors have the right to repeal bylaws (not in all states); declare dividends; and hire, fire, and compensate officers. However, a director does not have the right to amend the articles. (T) This right belongs to the shareholders.

V. Piercing the Corporate Veil

(The following methods have been tested. There are still other methods the AICPA can test)

A. Commingling

If a shareholder commingles his/her assets with the assets of the corporation, the corporate limited liability shield may be pierced. (TT)

May 1985 # 13

The corporate veil is most likely to be pierced and the shareholders held personally liable if

    a.   the corporation has elected S corporation status under the Internal Revenue Code.
    b.   a partnership incorporates its business solely to limit the liability of its partners.
    c.   an *ultra vires* act has been committed.
    d.   the shareholders have commingled their personal funds with those of the corporation.

CHAPTER 40   SECTION 5   PAGES 725-726

B.   Mere Formality

    If the shareholders do not act like a corporation (e.g. no record keeping, no meetings, no letterhead, etc.), then shield can be pierced. (TTT)

May 1982 # 8

A court is most likely to disregard the corporate entity and hold shareholders personally liable when

    a.   the owner-officers of the corporation do not treat it as a separate entity.
    b.   a parent corporation creates a wholly owned subsidiary in order to isolate the high risk portion of its business in the subsidiary.
    c.   a sole proprietor incorporates his/her business to limit his/her liability.
    d.   the corporation has elected, under Subchapter S, not to pay any corporate tax on its income but, instead, to have the shareholders pay tax on it.

CHAPTER 40   SECTION 5   PAGES 725-726

C.   Undercapitalization (T)

150 Business Law and the CPA Exam

VI. Shareholder Rights and Duties

   A. Shareholders have the right to <u>vote</u> on the following matters:

      1. Consolidation or merger with one or more corporations. (T)

      2. Voluntary dissolution. (T)

      3. Amending the Articles of Incorporation.

   B. Shareholders do <u>not</u> have the right to vote on:

      1. Purchase of 55% of another corporation's stock. (T)

      2. Short-form Merger (shareholder's parent corporation owns 90% of the subsidiary). (T)

   C. Inspection Rights

   The stockholder, unlike the director's near absolute right of inspection, has a <u>limited and reasonable</u> rights to inspect the corporate records. (T) The inspection must be for a <u>proper</u> purpose and should be made in advance. If the shareholder wants the corporate information for his/her own personal use, then the right will denied. (T)

   D. The shareholder, like a limited partner in a limited partnership, can freely transfer his/her interest/stock. (T)

VII. Dissolution

   A. Judicial

   A court can grant corporate dissolution, if the court finds a wasting of corporate assets. (T)

   B. The corporation can dissolve itself, with stockholder approval, by the Board's passage of a corporate resolution. (TT)

VII. Merger and Consolidation

   A. Merger requires approval of the corporate board of directors, a submission of the plan to the shareholders, and compliance with the 1933 Securities Act. (TTT)

> May 1984 #7
>
> Able and Baker are two corporations, the shares of which are publicly traded. Baker plans to merge into Able. Which of the following is a requirement of the merger?
>
>   a. The IRS must approve the merger.
>   b. The common stockholders of Baker must receive common stock of Able.
>   c. The creditors of Baker must approve the merger.
>   **d. The boards of directors of both Able and Baker must approve the merger.**
>
> CHAPTER 42   SECTION 1   PAGES 754-755

    B.   Merger can be a tax free reorganization under the IRS Code. (T)

    C.   Consolidation requirements include:

        1.   The board of directors of each corporation must adopt and approve. (T)

        2.   The shareholders must approve, and if any of the shareholders dissent, they must receive their appraisal rights. (T)

        3.   The Articles of Merger/Consolidation must be filed with the appropriate state officials.

ESSAY QUESTIONS

MAY, 1986 NUMBER 4
CORPORATE AND SHAREHOLDER LIABILITY

Issues Tested:

    I.   Piercing the Corporate Veil
    II.   *Respondeat Superior*
    III.   Watered Stock

A shareholder can be liable for corporate settings in several ways. First, a shareholder, or any person, is always liable for his/her own torts. Also, a shareholder can be liable for corporate torts, if the shareholder participated in the commission of the tort.

A shareholder may liable in contract or tort under the doctrine of "Piercing of the Corporate Veil." Here, the shareholder cannot escape personal liability for his/her actions. (See the multiple choice section for the reasons for piercing the veil.)

Under *respondeat superior*, the corporation will be strictly liable for the torts committed by its employees within the scope of the employee's employment.

The candidate should prepare to recognize and answer a question on watered stock. If a shareholder receives valuable corporate stock for worthless property, that shareholder has received "watered stock." The shareholder must pay damages.

NOVEMBER, 1987 NUMBER 5
CORPORATE FINANCE

Issues Tested:

    I.   Stated Capital
    II. Stock Splits/Dividends
    III. Dividends

As an aid to these essay questions you should resort to your accounting knowledge. Stated capital includes the par value for the shares. Also, under the old Model Business Code, organizational expenses can be considered as expenses and not charged to stated capital.

A stock dividend, while not effecting the market price, does increase stated capital. Likewise, the stock split will not affect stated capital, but instead have an impact on the stock's par value.

Cash dividends are not a liability until the Board declares the dividend. The Board can defend its failure to issue a dividend by employing the Business Judgement Rule. In any respect, the dividend may not be issued if the payment makes the corporation insolvent. The old Model Business Code states that net assets cannot be less than liabilities. States, GAAP/GAAS, and uniform statutes differ in their approach to surplus.

MAY, 1989 NUMBER 4
LIABILITY AND AUTHORITY OF THE BOARD

Issues Tested:

    I.   Liability
    II. Inspection Rights
    III. Officer Removal

Directors have extensive liability for their actions. However, the directors do have several powerful defenses. The director has the "Business Judgment Rule" as an effective defense. Directors, as well as officers, are <u>not</u> guarantors of business success. Therefore, the director cannot be held liable for his/her poor business judgement (e.g. his/her negligence). The director can argue that his/her errors were made in good faith, as another method of liability insulation. In fact, if a shareholder successively sues a director, the director can request indemnity. Here, while the "Business Judgement Rule" will not insulate the director from liability, the good faith defense will provide indemnity.

Because of the all the potential liability, the directors have almost unlimited inspection rights. The director should be able to inspect the corporate records in order to make more informed corporate judgements. The candidate should not confuse director inspection rights with shareholder inspection rights. Shareholders have limited inspection rights. The inspection must be for a proper purpose. A corporate competitor could not buy one share of stock and demand the right to inspect the competitor's formulas and client lists.

The right to hire, fire and compensate officers are rights of the directors. While the directors serve at the direction of the shareholders, officers serve at the pleasure of the directors. Therefore, a director can fire an officer with or without cause.

MAY, 1993 NUMBER 3
RIGHTS OF SHAREHOLDERS, DIRECTORS AND OFFICERS

Issues Tested:

   I.   Authority
   II. Fiduciary Duties
   III. Appraisal Rights

If a shareholder disapproves of certain corporate decisions, he/she may demand appraisal rights. With appraisal rights, a shareholder can force the corporation to purchase his/her shares of stock. The candidate should know the requirements. The requirements include written objection to the corporate action, voting against the corporate action, and submission for the right to a judge. This judge will determine the value of the shares, yet demand strict adherence to the appraisal requirements.

LONG OBJECTIVE QUESTIONS
MAY, 1995 NUMBER 2b
RIGHTS AND DUTIES OF STOCKHOLDERS, DIRECTORS, AND OFFICERS

Issues Tested:

I. Incorporation by statute
II. Initial bylaws adopted by directors
III. Directors elected by stockholders
IV. Directors appoint officers
V. Officers handle day to day operations
VI. Voting Agreements

SECURITIES REGULATION

Securities Regulation is an area of growing importance and CPA coverage. The candidate should take special note of this section, since Securities Regulation is one of the foundations for Accountant Liability. Therefore, these two sections should be studied in tandem.

However, this section is highly technical in scope, and the area of Exempt Transactions requires special attention.

I. Securities and Exchange Commission (SEC)

 A. The SEC does not criminally prosecute violations of the acts. This is the province of the Department of Justice. The SEC handles civil cases. (T)

November 1984 # 44

When there is evidence of a violation of the federal securities laws, the Securities and Exchange Commission lacks the power to

 a. subpoena witnesses.
 b. compel the production of books and records anywhere in the United States.
 c. order an administrative hearing to determine responsibility for the violation and impose certain sanctions.
 d. prosecute criminal cases.

CHAPTER 43   SECTION 1   PAGE 766

 B. Willful violations could result in a fine and imprisonment. (T)

 C. The anti-fraud provision of the 1933 and 1934 acts have criminal sanctions. (T)

 D. Reckless disregard for the truth can result in criminal sanctions. (T)

E. The SEC has the power to subpoena records, compel witnesses and conduct investigations. (T)

II. Securities Act of 1933 (Issuance of Stock)

The 1933 act was in response to the chaos created by the stock market crash in 1929. The candidate should remember this is an act of DISCLOSURE in the distribution of securities. Also, the 1933 act's mandate is to prevent fraud.

A. Coverage

1. The statute and courts provide a broad interpretation of the 1933 act. (T)

2. The 1933 act is an act of disclosure. The SEC will not judge the merits or the success of the offering. (T)

B. Registration Statement/Process

1. The prospectus is part of the registration process. (T)

2. A "red herring" is a preliminary prospectus. (T)

3. The "tombstone ads" can be printed, after the waiting period, to inform potential investors where they can find a prospectus. (T)

4. Registration requirements include: (TT)

May 1993

Which of the following disclosures must be contained in a securities registration statement filed under the Securities Act of 1933?

a. A list of all existing stockholders.
b. The principal purposes for which the offering proceeds will be used.
c. A copy of the corporation's latest proxy solicitation statement.
d. The names of all prospective accredited investors.

CHAPTER 43   SECTION 2   PAGE 767

a. Description of the issuer's/registrant's business and properties.

b. Description of the security

c. Capital structure of the business

d. Amount of the proceeds and their use

e. Underwriting arrangements

f. Certified financial statements

g. Signatures

5. Once the registration is filed, oral or written offers may be made. The offers may be extended throughout the twenty day waiting period. No sale can be consummated until the SEC provides an effective date. (T)

6. Security

The definition of a SECURITY can mean almost anything (e.g. worms). Any definition of a security must begin with the *Howey* case. The U.S. Supreme Court defined a security (in this case an investment contract in orange groves) as a transaction or scheme whereby a person 1) invests his/her money, 2) in a common enterprise, 3) with the reasonable expectation of profit, 4) solely from the managerial efforts of others. (T) Although, the CPA exam does not test directly on this definition, the candidate should be able to apply the definition to a specific testing situation (e.g. a negotiable corporate note[T]).

May 1993 #30

Which of the following is least likely to be considered a security under the Securities Act of 1933?

a. Stock options.
b. Warrants.
c. General partnership interests.
d. Limited partnership interests.

CHAPTER 43   SECTION 2   PAGE 767

158   Business Law and the CPA Exam

C. Exempt Securities

Since the registration is time consuming and costly, registrants attempt to reduce their costs with exempt securities or exempt transactions.

1. The AICPA has tested on the following exempt securities—municipal government securities, not-for-profit entities or charities, banks, and solely intrastate offerings. (T) Stock warrants are <u>not</u> exempt. (T)

2. Regulation A

Reg A has been comprehensively revised by the SEC. Reg. A securities have a simpler and less costly registration process. Up to $5 million of securities can be offered in a twelve-month period, yet subject to a $1.5 million maximum for secondary offerings. Reg. A allows smaller companies to "test the water" with a "offering circular," not a prospectus, for potential investors. (WT)

D. Exempt Transactions

During the last few years, the SEC has designed and redesigned the laws to allow small businesses an easier time in offering securities. In essence the SEC abdicated enforcement to the states with the exemptions. The candidate should learn the exemptions in Reg. D and the corresponding Rules.

1. Rule 504 of Regulation D

May 1992 # 44

Data, Inc. intends to make a $375,000 common stock offering under Rule 504 of Regulation D of the Securities Act of 1933. Data

a. may sell the stock to an unlimited number of investors.
b. may not make the offering through a general advertising.
c. must offer the stock for a period of more than 12 months.
d. must provide all investors with a prospectus.

CHAPTER 43   SECTION 2   PAGE 768-769

---

a. Noninvestment company offerings up to $1 million in any 12-month period are exempt. (TT)

b. The SEC must be notified of the sale. (T)

c. Under 504a of Reg. D, offerings up to $500,000 in any one year by "blank check" companies are exempt, if no general solicitation or advertising is used. (T)

2. Rule 505 of Reg. D

a. Private, noninvestment company offerings up to $5 million in any 12-month period are exempt, regardless of the number of ACCREDITED investors. (TT) Accredited investors are those investors who because of their high net worth or position (banks, insurance companies, etc.) do not need the protection of the disclosure rules.

May 1993 # 17

Regulation D of the Securities Act of 1933

a. restricts the number of purchasers of an offering to 35.
b. permits an exempt offering to be sold to both accredited and unaccredited investors.
c. is limited to offers and sales of common stock that do not exceed $1.5 million.
d. is exclusively available to small business corporations as defined by Regulation D.

CHAPTER 43   SECTION 2   PAGE 768-769

---

b. The exemption is applicable up to 35 unaccredited investors. (T)

c. Audited financial statements must be supplied to the unaccredited investors. (T)

d. The SEC must be notified of the sale. (T)

3. Rule 506 of Reg. D (a.k.a. Private Placement)

a. Private noninvestment company offerings in unlimited amounts that are not generally solicited or advertised (e.g. not an offering to the public) are exempt. (TT)

160 Business Law and the CPA Exam

> May 1989 #45
>
> Maco Limited Partnership intends to sell $6,000,000 of its limited partnership interests. The state in which Maco was organized is also the state in which it carries on all of its business activities.
>
> If Maco intends to offer the limited partnership interests in reliance on Rule 506 of Regulation D under the Securities Act of 1933 to prospective investors residing in several states, which of the following statements is correct?
>
> a. The offering will be exempt from the anti-fraud provisions of the Securities Exchange Act of 1934.
> b. Any subsequent resale of a limited partnership interest by a purchaser will be exempt from registration.
> **c. Maco may make an unlimited number of offers to sell the limited partnership interests.**
> d. No more than 35 purchasers may acquire the limited partnership interests.
>
> CHAPTER 43   SECTION 2   PAGES 768-769

        b.   The SEC must be notified of the sale. (T)

        c.   There can no more than 35 unaccredited investors. (T)

        d.   If there are any unaccredited investors, then these investors must be provided with "material information" (e.g. audited financial statements). (T)

    4.   Rule 147 (Intrastate Transactions)

        a.   Rule 147 exempts intrastate transactions involving local offerings. (T)

        b.   For 9 months after the last sale, The SEC imposes restrictions on resale. For 9 months after the last sale, there can be resale to nonresidents. (T)

E.   Civil Liability under the 1933 act. (See also the section on Accountant Liability.)

    1.   The SEC and the victims can sue for fraud. (T)

2. An accountant can defend him/herself with a showing of due diligence. (T)

3. The plaintiff need only show that he/she purchased the stock and suffered a loss. This is <u>not</u> a fraud standard. Therefore, the plaintiff does not have to show reliance. (T)

III. Securities and Exchange Act of 1934 (Exchanges of Stock)

    A. Coverage

The 1934 act is similar to the 1933 act, since this act is also an act of disclosure. In addition, the act's mandate is to prevent fraud. However, it is different from the 1933 act because, while the 1933 act covers the issuance of securities, the 1934 act governs exchanges.

        1. Violations of the act can result in a prison term. (T)

        2. This act covers transactions for shares listed on national security exchanges, tender offers, insider trading and the solicitation of proxies. (TT)

        3. The AICPA still tests on the definition of security. A security could be an investment contracts, debenture (convertible and non-convertible), etc. However, a bank C.D. is not a security. (T)

        4. The act requires an annual 10-K report. (TT)

        5. The disclosures include bonuses, financial reports, profit sharing arrangements, the names of officers, directors and large stock holders, etc. Significant specific events must also be disclosed. Testable areas include: new auditors, new officers and directors, defaults and bankruptcy.

        6. The 1934 act also has limits. The act governs companies with assets in excess of $5 million and 500 or more shareholders. (TT)

    B. Anti-Fraud and Insider Trader Provisions

The candidate should be aware that this section receives extensive testing in Accountant Liability.

        1. Even if the company is exempt from the 1934 act, the anti-fraud rules of the 1933 act still apply. (T)

2. Section 10(b)

In this section the SEC prohibits "any manipulative or deceptive device or contrivance in contravention of the such rules (e.g. 10b-5) and regulations" prescribed by the SEC based on interstate transactions. (TT)

3. Rule 10b-5

This rule is more specific than Section 10(b).

a. Rule 10b-5 establishes liability on those (e.g. accountants) who mislead, deceptively misrepresent or omit material facts in connection with the purchase or sale of securities. (T)

b. Again, it is recommended that the candidate study the elements of the tort of fraud. For example, the CPA Exam will expect that the applicant knows that <u>scienter</u> is an element of fraud (and 10b-5). (T)

c. The 1934 act also imposes liability on tipper/tippees who use inside information, and on outsiders who misappropriate material nonpublic information. (TT)

November 1993 #42

Which of the following persons is not an insider of a corporation subject to the Securities Exchange Act of 1934 registration and reporting requirements?

a. An attorney for the corporation.
b. **An owner of 5% of the corporation's outstanding debentures.**
c. A member of the board of directors.
d. A stockholder who owns 10% of the outstanding common stock.

CHAPTER 43   SECTION 3   PAGES 772-773

---

d. Section 16(b)

Officers, directors and shareholders with more than 10% of stock must file reports with the SEC and are liable for short swing gains. (T)

f. Section 14(a)

Those who solicit proxies from shareholders must make full disclosure to the SEC. (T)

C. State Securities Law

Each state has their own "Blue Sky" Laws, and there is no automatic state exemption with a SEC filing (T)

ESSAY QUESTIONS

MAY, 1981 NUMBER 4
FOREIGN CONTRACTS

Issues Tested:

    I. Securities and Exchange Act of 1934
    II. Foreign Corrupt Practices Act

NOVEMBER, 1981 NUMBER 2
CORPORATE MERGER

Issues Tested:

    I. Securities Act of 1933
    II. Merger Requirements

MAY, 1982 NUMBER 2
SECURITIES REGISTRATION

Issues Tested:

    I. Registration Requirements of the Securities Act of 1933

NOVEMBER, 1982 NUMBER 4
PROXY FIGHT

Issues Tested:

    I. Access to Shareholder Lists
    II. Securities and Exchange Act of 1934

MAY, 1983 NUMBER 3
CORPORATE MERGER

Issues Tested:

    I.   Merger
    II.   Securities and Exchange Act of 1934

NOVEMBER, 1985 NUMBER 5
"GOING PUBLIC" TO RAISE FUNDS

Issues Tested:
    I.   Registration under the 1933 Act
    II.   Reg. D and Rule 505

NOVEMBER, 1992 NUMBER 2
ISSUANCE/EXEMPTIONS OF SECURITIES UNDER 1933 ACT

Issues Tested:

    I.   Rule 504 of Reg. D
    II.   Rule 505 of Reg. D
    III. Rule 506 of Reg. D

The candidate will be tested on the exemptions in Reg. D.

I.   Rule 504 of Reg. D

    A.   The exemption applies to noninvestment company interstate offerings up to $1,000,000 in any 12-month period.

    B.   Rule 504a places the limit at $500,000 in any year by "blank check" companies. These companies have no specific business plan except to find and acquire unknown business opportunities.

    C.   The SEC must be notified within 15 days of the sale.

II.   Rule 505 of Reg. D

    A.   Private, noninvestment company offerings up to $5,000,000 in any 12-month period are exempt.

> B. The sale is limited to 35 unaccredited investors, but may be solicited to an unlimited number of accredited investors.
>
> C. The SEC must be notified within 15 days of the sale.

III. Rule 506 (Private Placement) of Reg. D

> A. Private, noninvestment company offerings of up to $5,000,000 in any 12-month period are exempt, if the offering is not generally advertised or solicited (private placement).
>
> B. The sale is limited to 35 unaccredited investors, but may be solicited to an unlimited number of accredited investors.
>
> C. The SEC must be notified within 15 days of the sale.

LONG OBJECTIVE QUESTIONS
May, 1994 NUMBERS 61-65

Issues Tested:

> I. Section 11 of Securities Act of 1933 and 10(b) and Rule 10b-5 the Securities Exchange Act of 1934
> II. Defenses to the above

MAY, 1995 NUMBER 5
PUBLIC OFFERING OF STOCK

Issues Tested:

> I. Reg. D and Rule 505
> II. Resale under Reg. D
> III. Requirements of the 1934 Act
> IV. SEC Reporting requirements

LONG OBJECTIVE QUESTIONS
NOVEMBER, 1995 NUMBER 3b
PRIVATE PLACEMENT OFFERING

Issues Tested:

> I. Reg.D Exemption under Rule 506
> II. SEC Notification

INVESTMENT SECURITIES
UCC ARTICLE 8

This section is not to be confused with Federal Securities Law under the 1933 and 1934 acts. The UCC is uniform <u>state</u> law. The candidate should spend much more time on federal securities law than in the state area. The questions under Article 8 are few and predictable.

I. Definition

    A. Security

        Under 8-102 a SECURITY is defined as a "share, participation, or other interest in property or an enterprise of the issuer or an obligation of the issuer." (WTT) There are two types of securities:

November 1983 # 48

In order to qualify as an investment security under the Uniform Commercial Code, an instrument must be

    a.   issued in registered form, and not the bearer form.
    b.   of a long-term nature not intended to be disposed of within one year.
    c.   only an equity security or debenture security, and not a secured obligation.
    d.   in a form that evidences a share, participation or other interest in property or in an enterprise, or evidences an obligation of the issuer.

CHAPTER N/A   SECTION N/A   PAGE N/A

---

        1.   Certified

a. Registered Form

Specifies a person who is entitled to the investment security. (WT)

b. Bearer Form

"Runs to bearer according to its terms and not by reason of any indorsement." This type of security is rarely, if ever, tested.

2. Uncertified

This type of security is rarely, if ever, tested.

B. BFP (Bona Fide Purchaser) 8-302(1)

A BFP is a purchaser for value, in good faith, and without notice of any adverse claim. The BFP can take delivery of the security in bearer form, or in registered form, or indorsed to the BFP, or in blank. (WT)

1. A BFP takes security free from adverse title claims. (T)

II. Rights and Restrictions of Issuance

A. A valid certified security is entitled to reissue. (WT)

B. The sale of the security requires a stated quantity at a definite price. (WT)

C. Any restrictions on the sale of the security must appear on the face of the security. (WT) See, also, Article 3 on negotiability.

November 1992 # 44

Under the UCC Investment Securities Article, a restriction on the transfer of corporate stock will only be valid against a transferee if the restriction is

a. contained in a stockholders' agreement.
b. **stated on the face of the stock certificate.**
c. placed on publicly traded stock.
d. part of a buy-sell contract.

CHAPTER N/A   SECTION N/A   PAGE N/A

D. A holder of a security is entitled to a replacement of a lost certificate: (WT)

1. Before a BFP receives the security.

2. If the true owner files an indemnity bond with the issuer.

3. If the owner satisfies any reasonable requirements (e.g. notifying the issuer within a reasonable time).

III. Warranties

Just as in Article 3, Article 8 of the UCC provides warranties. The candidate should study the transfer warranties under 8-306(2) which states: (TT)

" A person by transferring a certified security to a purchaser for value warrants only that:

1. Transfer is effective and rightful;

2. The security is genuine and has not been materially altered; and

3. The person knows of no fact which might impair the validity of the security."

May 1985 #40

Unless otherwise agreed, which of the following warranties will not be conferred by a person negotiating a negotiable warehouse receipt for value to his/her immediate purchaser?

    a. The document is genuine.
    b. The transferor is without knowledge of any fact which would impair its validity or worth.
    c. The goods represented by the warehouse receipt are of merchantable
    d. Negotiation by the transferor is rightful and fully effective with respect to the title to the document.

CHAPTER N/A   SECTION N/A   PAGE N/A

There are other, yet rarely tested, warranties under the Article 8.

ESSAY QUESTION

NOVEMBER, 1989 NUMBER 5
SHAREHOLDER RIGHTS

Issues Tested:

- I. Cumulative Preferred Stock
- II. Shareholder's Right of Inspection
- III. Stock Certificate Replacement

The AICPA rarely tests on documents of title and investment securities. In fact, the rare essay question contains one investment security issue.

As discussed in corporate law, cumulative preferred stock is not a liability until a dividend is declared. Also, a shareholder has no absolute right to inspection. The request must be for a proper purpose.

Finally, since a stock certificate is a representation of the shareholder's personal property right, the shareholder can request a duplicate certificate under the rule of Article 8 of the UCC.

Documents of Title (Warehouse Receipts, Bills of Lading, and Others) UCC Article 7

This section of the UCC is not as thoroughly tested as the other articles of the UCC. In addition, *West's Business Law* concentrates more in the heavily tested UCC areas. However, Article 7 is very closely aligned with Article 3 in terms of negotiability, transfer and liability. If the candidate forgets the rules of Article 7, he/she can revert back to Article 3 and still be generally correct.

I. Definitions

   A. Warehouse Receipt

   According to UCC 1-201(45) a WAREHOUSE RECEIPT is a type of a document of title issued by a person engaged in the business of storing goods for hire. (TT)

   B. Bill of Lading

   According to UCC 1-201(16) a BILL OF LADING is a document of title evidencing the receipt of goods for shipment issued by a person engaged in the business of transporting goods. This would be a carrier, not a consignee. (TT)

II. Negotiability

   A. A document of title, under UCC 7-104(1)(a), is negotiable if it provides that goods are to be delivered to the bearer (bearer document) or to the order of a named person (order document). (TT)

> May 1993 # 44
>
> Under the UCC, a bill of lading
>
>   a.   will never be enforceable if altered.
>   b.   is issued by a consignee of goods.
>   c.   will never be negotiable unless it is endorsed.
>   **d.   is negotiable if the goods are to be delivered to the bearer.**
>
> CHAPTER 43   SECTION 2   PAGES 373-374

    B.   A holder under Article 7 differs from a holder in Article 3 in a few respects. First, an Article 7 holder by definition is one who purchased the document in good faith, for value and without notice of any defenses against or claims to it. Therefore, the Article 7 holder does not have all the requirements of a HDC in Article 3. Also, while an antecedent debt can be "value" under Article 3, Article 7 requires present value. (WTTT)

III.   Transfer or Negotiation

    A.   Just like Article 3, Article 7 defines the transfer of a nonnegotiable document (Article 3 says "instrument") as a contract law assignment. (WTT)

    B.   The proper negotiation or transfer of an order document requires endorsement and delivery. (TT)

    C.   The proper negotiation or transfer of a bearer document requires delivery alone. (TT)

    D.   A forged signature (endorsement) does not pass good title. (TT)

III.   Liability of Endorser or Transferor

    A.   Unlike Article 3, the endorser of a negotiable document of title does not obtain liability for the bailee's failure to perform, but they do make warranties similar to Article 3. These warranties include that the document is genuine, that there is no knowledge of any fact that would impair value, and that transfer is rightful. (WT)

    B.   The importance of negotiability is that the holder of such a document can receive, hold, and dispose of the document or the goods. In fact, the good-faith purchaser may acquire greater rights to the document or the goods than the transferor had or had the

Documents of Title: UCC Article 7   173

authority to convey. (TT) Article 7 does not call such a person a "HDC," but this status provides nearly the same function.

C. A negotiable warehouse receipt allows the warehouse person to commingle the goods with other fungible goods. (WTT)

May 1984 # 46

Woody Pyle, a public warehouseman, issued Merlin a negotiable warehouse receipt for fungible goods stored. Pyle

    a. may not limit the amount of his liability for his own negligence.
    b. will be absolutely liable for any damages in the absence of a statute or a provision on the warehouse receipt to the contrary.
    c. may commingle Merlin's goods with similar fungible goods of other bailors.
    d. is obligated to deliver the goods to Merlin despite Merlin's improper refusal to pay the storage charges due.

CHAPTER N/A   SECTION N/A   PAGE N/A

D. With a warehouse receipt, there is no need to notify the warehouse before valid negotiation. (WT)

E. A negotiable warehouse receipt given to thieves by the warehouse person is ineffective to pass title. (WT)

IV. Duty of Care

A. A warehouse person has a duty to use reasonable care (e.g. negligence is the standard). In addition, this liability can be limited by contract. (TT)

May 1983 # 44

Under the Uniform Commercial Code's rule, a warehouseman

    a. is liable as an insurer.
    b. will not be liable for the nonreceipt or misdescription of the goods stored even to a good-faith purchaser for value of a warehouse receipt.

> c. cannot limit its liability with respect to loss or damage to goods while in its possession.
>
> **d. is liable for damages which could have been avoided through the exercise of due care.**
>
> CHAPTER 43   SECTION 3   PAGES 378-380
> CHAPTER 49   SECTION 6   PAGES 885-888

    B.   A common carrier has a strict liability standard. (T)

V.   Risk of Loss

    A.   When title is to be transferred by a negotiable document of title without the movement of goods, risk of loss passes to the transferee, with the goods at the time of receipt. (T) See Article 2 rules.

ESSAY QUESTIONS

The AICPA rarely, if ever, tests on Documents of Title in the essay section.

PROPERTY (REAL AND PERSONAL)

I. Personal Property

The CPA Exam tests much more on the candidate's knowledge of real property than of personal property.

   A. Differences between real and personal property

   1. A deed transfers real property, while a sale or gift transfers personal property. (T)

   2. A creditor exercises his/her right with foreclosure on real property, but with repossession on personal property. (T)

   3. A fixture is personal property that becomes affixed to real property with the intent to become part of the real property. Another test is that the personal property remains personal property, even after attachment, if the item can be removed without damage. (TTT)

May 1985 # 51

Which of the following factors is <u>least</u> significant in determining whether an item of personal property has become a fixture?

   a. The value of the item.
   b. The manner of attachment.
   c. The adaptability of the item to the real estate.
   d. The extent of injury which would be caused to the real property by the removal of the item.

CHAPTER 48   SECTION 2   PAGES 863-864

4. Shares of stock, trademarks, copyrights, patents and promissory notes etc. are NOT tangible personal property, but represent INTANGIBLE personal property rights. (T)

5. A finder of abandoned personal property can claim ownership of this property. (T)

B. Concurrent Property Ownership

1. Tenancy in Common

   a. Creation

   A form of co-ownership in which two or more persons own an undivided interest in the whole property. (T)

   b. Transfer

   The AICPA rarely tests directly in this area. It tests more on joint tenancy. But a candidate should be aware that a tenancy in common interest, unlike joint tenancy, can be transferred in a will. (TT)

2. Joint Tenancy (with Rights of Survivorship)

   a. Creation

   1) A form of co-ownership in which two or more persons own an equal undivided interest in the whole property. (T)

   2) In order to create joint tenancy, all joint tenants must receive all of the Four Unities (Time, Title, Interest and Possession). Therefore, joint tenants must possess both interest and title at the same time). (WT)

May 1993 # 52

Which of the following unities (elements) are required to establish a joint tenancy?

	Time	Title	Interest	Possession
a.	**Yes**	**Yes**	**Yes**	**Yes**

b.	Yes	Yes	No	No
c.	No	No	Yes	Yes
d.	Yes	No	Yes	No

CHAPTER N/A   SECTION N/A   PAGE N/A

    b.   Deed Transfers

If a joint tenant transfers his/her interest (by deed) to a third party, then that third party will be a tenant in common with the remaining joint tenant(s). (T) The remaining joint tenants are still joint tenants between or among themselves. (T)

    c.   Will Transfers

A joint tenant cannot transfer his/her interest by will. The remaining tenants receive his/her interest by the right of survivorship. (TT) This rule does not apply to corporations. (WTT)

November 1988 # 56

Green and Nunn own a 40-acre parcel of land as joint tenants with the right of survivorship. Nunn wishes to sell the land to Ink. If Nunn alone executes and delivers a deed to Ink, what will be the result?

   a.   **Green will retain a 1/2 undivided interest in the 40-acre parcel, and will be unable to set aside Nunn's conveyance to Ink.**
   b.   Ink will obtain an interest in 1/2 of the parcel, or 20 acres.
   c.   Ink will share ownership of the 40 acres with Green as a joint tenant with a right of survivorship.
   d.   The conveyance will be invalid because Green did <u>not</u> sign the deed.

CHAPTER 48   SECTION 3   PAGE 865

II.   Bailments

Bailments have rarely been tested, yet bailments were tested in 1994.

A. Element of a Bailment

    1. Personal Property

    2. Delivery of the property, without title, from bailor to bailee.

    3. Absolute duty on bailee to return the personal property. (T)

III. Real Property

    A. Easements (rarely tested)

One way to obtain an easement is by prescription. Prescription is another term for adverse possession. The candidate should know the elements of adverse possession.

    1. Actual and Exclusive

    2. Open, Visible, and Notorious

    3. Continuous

    4. Hostile and Adverse (T)

    B. Transfer by Deed (Elements of)

November 1990 # 54

For a deed to be effective between the purchaser and seller of real estate, one of the conditions is that the deed must

    a. contain the signatures of the seller and purchaser.
    b. contain the actual sales price.
    c. be delivered by the seller with an intent to transfer title.
    d. be recorded within the permissible statutory time limits.

CHAPTER 50   SECTION 3   PAGE 896

---

    1. Name of the Grantor and Grantee (T)

    2. Intent of the Grantor to Convey (TT)

3. Legal Description (TTT)

4. Signed by the party to be charged. (Grantor—this is a requirement under the state's Statute of Frauds) (T)

5. Delivery (T) and Acceptance

C. Elements of a deed do not include:

1. Consideration (TT)

2. Signatures of both the Grantor and Grantee (TT)

3. Recording

   A recording is not required for the deed to be valid between the grantor (seller) and the grantee (buyer). (T) See the Recording Statutes for the law concerning third parties.

4. The Purchase Price (T)

D. Types of Deeds (The AICPA does not test on every type of deed, but on the most common.)

1. General Warranty Deed

   a. Protection

      Provides the greatest number of covenants and protection for the buyer. (T)

   b. Covenants include: (T)

      1) Right to own and convey (seizin)

      2) Quiet enjoyment (no disturbances)

      3) No encumbrances

      4) Further assurances

2. Quitclaim

180 Business Law and the CPA Exam

QUITCLAIM deeds provide little protection for the grantee-buyer. The grantee-buyer only receives the interest that his/her grantor-seller has in the property. (T)

E. Recording Statutes

The RECORDING STATUTES are a favorite topic of the CPA Exam. The candidate should not become intimidated by these acts. First, the candidate should understand that the purpose of the recording statutes is to answer the priority problem of two deeds on the same property. Will the holder of the deed then have priority over a subsequent grantee who paid value and did not know about the grantee's earlier conveyance? (The law calls the good-faith purchaser a BFP. The law loves to protect the BFP who pays value.) If the grantee records his/her interest, the BFP is on constructive notice of this conveyance and the BFP will lose priority. (TTT)

May 1983 # 58

Recordation of a real property mortgage

    a. is required to validate the rights of the parties to the mortgage.
    b. will **not** be effective if improperly filed even if the party claiming superior title had actual notice of its existence.
    c. perfects the interest of the mortgage against subsequent bona fide purchasers for value.
    d. must be filed in the recordation office where the mortgagee's principal place of business is located.

CHAPTER 50   SECTION 3   PAGES 898-899

---

    1. Therefore, the candidate should be aware of the three different recording statutes.

        a. Race (rarely, if ever tested—too easy)

        b. Race-Notice

        The BFP will have priority over the earlier conveyance, if the BFP recorded first <u>and</u> without notice of the earlier conveyance. (WTT)

Property 181

May 1990 # 55

On February 2, Mazo deeded a warehouse to Parko for $450,000. Parko did not record the deed. On February 12, Mazo deeded the same warehouse to Nexis for $430,000. Nexis was aware of the prior conveyance to Parko. Nexis recorded its deeds before Parko recorded. Who would prevail under the following recording status?

	Notice Statute	Race Statute	Race-Notice Statute
a.	Nexis	Parko	Parko
b.	**Parko**	**Nexis**	**Parko**
c.	Parko	Nexis	Nexis
d.	Parko	Parko	Nexis

CHAPTER 50   SECTION 3   PAGES 898-899

---

    c.   Pure Notice

The BFP will have priority over the earlier conveyance if the BFP received his/her deed without notice of the earlier conveyance.

F.   Sale of Real Property

In a Contract for Sale, the parties will put certain conditions that must be met before the buyer's duty to pay begins. (T) (In contract law these conditions are called "conditions precedent." A typical condition in a Contract for Sale would be a reasonable effort to find financing.) The sale of real property is most likely to be an arm's length transaction. (T)

G.   Title Insurance

A TITLE INSURANCE policy protects the home buyer from defects in the home's title. The insurance company must defend the home buyer and pay the cost and the damages caused by the defects. (T)

    1.   An unrecorded easement is a defect in the marketable title of the property. (T)

    2.   Another way to describe this defect is as a breach of the Implied Warranty of

182   Business Law and the CPA Exam

Marketability. (T)

3. Title Insurance is normally not transferable. (WTT)

May 1993 # 54

A standard title insurance policy will generally insure that

a. there are <u>no</u> other deeds to the property.
b. **the purchaser has good record title as of the policy's date.**
c. all taxes and assessments are paid.
d. the insurance protection will be transferrable to a subsequent purchaser.

CHAPTER 50   SECTION 3   PAGE 901

H. Mortgage

The MORTGAGE is the promise the borrower makes to the lender. The borrower pledges the home as collateral for the home loan. The candidate should keep in mind that, since the borrower is making the promise, he/she is called the "mortgagor," and the receiver of the promise, the bank, is known as the "mortgagee." The AICPA will probably not test directly on these definitions, but will assume the candidate knows the difference.

1. Requirements

The requirements are the same as the elements of a deed. Testable subjects have included:

a. The mortgage requires a writing under the Statute of Frauds. (WTT) The mortgage should be signed by the party to be charged (the mortgagor). (WT)

November 1986 # 53

Which of the following statements is correct with respect to real estate mortgage?

a. **It must be signed only by the mortgagor (borrower).**

> b. It must be recorded in order to be effective between the mortgagor and mortgagee.
> c. It does <u>not</u> have to be recorded to be effective against third parties without notice if it is a purchase money mortgage.
> d. It is effective even if <u>not</u> delivered to the mortgagee.
>
> CHAPTER N/A   SECTION N/A   PAGE N/A

   b. If the mortgage is not recorded there could be a priority problem with a subsequent BFP. However, the failure to record has no effect between the original parties (mortgagor and the mortgagee). (WT)

   c. The mortgage should contain the legal description of the property. (WTT)

 2. Transfer

   a. Unless otherwise stated, the mortgage is freely transferable. (WT)

   b. While the note requires the rate and the amount of the debt, the mortgage does not. (T)

   c. There can be no transfer of title without the mortgage. (WT)

   d. Assuming versus Taking the Property Subject to the Mortgage:

   Candidates should understand the differences between "assuming" a mortgage and taking the property "subject to" the mortgage. This distinction will also become important in Landlord/Tenant Law.

    1) If the assignee assumes the mortgage, the assignee will be liable. If the buyer takes property "subject to" the mortgage, then the transferee is not liable on the mortgage. (WT)

    2) With an assumption, the mortgagor is still liable on the mortgage. This is because the mortgagor is still in privity of contract with the mortgagee, and a release or novation is required to remove the liability.

 3. Foreclosure (W)

   a. Mortgagor's Rights at Default/Foreclosure

184   Business Law and the CPA Exam

        1)   The right to redeem the property. There are two rights of redemption: The Equitable Right of Redemption and the Statutory Right of Redemption. With the right of redemption, the mortgagor may have a year to pay the amount due on the mortgage, costs and interest. (WTT)

May 1993 #58

A mortgagor's right of redemption will be terminated by a judicial foreclosure sale unless the

    a.   proceeds from the sale are <u>not</u> sufficient to fully satisfy the mortgage debt.
    b.   mortgage instrument does <u>not</u> provide for a default sale.
    c.   mortgagee purchases the property for market value.
    d.   jurisdiction has enacted a statutory right of redemption.

CHAPTER N/A   SECTION N/A   PAGE N/A

---

        2)   The right to refinance. (T)

        3)   The right to receive surplus at foreclosure.

        4)   The right to notice of the foreclosure.

    b.   Priority

        1)   At a judicial foreclosure the foreclosure costs are paid first and then the mortgage debt. Mortgagor is entitled to any surplus, yet liable for any deficiency. (WT)

        2)   If there are two mortgages on the property and the second mortgage is foreclosed, the proceeds go first to pay the first mortgage. (WTT)

May 1981 #54

Tremont Enterprises, Inc. needed some additional working capital to develop a new product line. It decided to obtain intermediate term financing by giving a second mortgage on its plant and warehouse. Which of the following is true with respect to

> the mortgages?
>
> a. If Tremont defaults on both the mortgages and a bankruptcy proceeding is initiated, the second mortgagee has the status of general creditor.
> b. **If the second mortgagee proceeds to foreclose on its mortgage, the first mortgagee must be satisfied completely before the second mortgagee is entitled to repayment.**
> c. Default on payment to the second mortgagee will constitute default on the first mortgage.
> d. Tremont <u>cannot</u> prepay the second mortgage prior to its maturity without the consent of the first mortgagee.
>
> CHAPTER N/A   SECTION N/A   PAGE N/A

    4. The Real Estate Settlement Procedures Act (RESPA) regulates mortgage lenders. (WT)

III. Landlord-Tenant Relationships

    A. Elements of a Lease

        1. Requirements

            a. The lease should be in writing, since the lease is an interest in land which is covered by the Statute of Frauds. However, in some jurisdictions (and on the CPA Exam) a six-month oral lease is enforceable. (TT)

            b. The lease provides the tenant with temporary possession of the property. (T)

            c. The lease should provide the duration of the lease and reserve the reversion for the landlord. (T)

            d. If the lease is silent, the payment is to be made at the end of the lease. (WT)

            e. A residential lease should include a description of leased premises and the due date for payment. (TT)

        2. Transfer

a. The tenant has the right to assign/sublet, unless this right is limited by statute. (T) The landlord must be reasonable in the denial of transfer.

b. If the tenant transfers only part of the lease, this is called a sublease. If the tenant transfers the whole lease term, this is called an assignment. (TT)

c. The tenant is still liable in contract to the landlord despite the transfer. (TT)

November 1988 # 57

Tell, Inc, leased a building from Lott Corp. Tell paid monthly rent of $500 and was also responsible for paying the building's real estate taxes. On January 1, 1987, Vorn Co. and Tell entered into an agreement by which Vorn was entitled to occupy the building for monthly payments of $600 to Tell. For the year 1987, neither Tell nor Vorn paid the delinquent taxes. Both refused to do so, and Lott has commenced an action against them. Lott will most likely prevail against

a. Vorn because the lease was assigned to it.
b. Tell and Vorn because both are jointly and severally liable for the delinquent taxes.
c. **Tell without Vorn because their January 1 agreement constituted a sublease.**
d. Vorn, but only to the extent of $100 for each month that it occupied the building during 1987.

CHAPTER 51   SECTION 4   PAGES 920-921

---

3. Termination of the Lease

a. The lease terminates when the time period expires. (T)

b. The lease terminates if the purpose of the lease fails. (T)

c. The lease could also terminate under a doctrine called "merger." If the tenant ever purchases the property from the landlord, then the tenant's lease merges with the landlord's reversion and the lease is gone. (T) The merger doctrine also terminates a trust or an easement.

B. Nonfreehold Estates

1. Estate for Years

    The landlord and tenant agree in the lease that duration of the lease will be for a <u>specific</u> time (months, years, etc.). (T)

2. Periodic Tenancy

    The landlord and tenant do <u>not</u> agree on a specific duration of the lease. Therefore, the lease automatically continues from period to period until terminated by proper notice. (T)

3. Tenancy at Will

    The landlord and tenant agree that either party can terminate the leasehold at any time. (T)

4. Tenancy at Sufferance

    The tenant wrongfully stays beyond the lease period. This tenant is also known as a "holdover," while the landlord "suffers" his/her presence. (T)

IV. Environmental Protection

This is a recent area of testing. The candidate should be forewarned that further questions are possible.

A. Remedies

   The EPA has several remedies for violations of the environmental protection laws. These remedies include injunctive relief and the right of the state or the citizenry to sue for money damages. (T)

B. Present owners, past owners and transporters can be liable under the Comprehensive Environmental Response, Compensation, and Liability Act. (WT)

C. The Clean Water Act regulates water that is discharged by nuclear power plants, the dredging of wetlands. (T)

ESSAY QUESTIONS

NOVEMBER, 1984 NUMBER 2
THE SALE OF A MANUFACTURING PLANT

Issues Tested:

    I.   Taking Property Subject to the Mortgage
    II.   Taking the Property by Assuming the Mortgage
    III.   Release by Novation
    IV.   Anti-assignment Clauses

Joe Fine, a clothing manufacturer for the past 30 years, owns a plant on which Muni Bank holds a mortgage. He also leases a warehouse from Jay Co. in which he stores the clothing manufactured in the plant. There are 10 years remaining on the lease term. Fine plans to move his operations to another location and has decided to sell to Bean his interest in the plant and the lease.

Fine is contemplating selling the plant to Bean under one of the following conditions:

    1.   Bean taking the plant subject to the mortgage.

    2.   Bean assuming the mortgage on the plant.

    3.   Fine obtaining a duly executed novation from Muni and Bean.

The lease contains a clause prohibiting assignment to third parties. Fine is concerned with this clause, as well as his continuing liability to Jay upon the transfer of his interests in the lease to Bean. In this regard, Fine asserts that:

    1.   The clause prohibiting the assignment of the lease is void.

    2.   The prohibition against assignment will not affect his right to sublease.

    3.   He will be released from liability to pay rent upon obtaining Jay's consent either to sublet or to assign.

REQUIRED:

Answer the following, setting forth reasons for any conclusions stated.

    1.   In separate paragraphs, discuss Fine's and Bean's liability to Muni under each of the three aforementioned conditions relating to the mortgage if Bean, after purchasing

the plant, defaults on the mortgage payments, thereby creating a deficiency after a foreclosure sale.

2. In separate paragraphs, comment on Fine's assertions regarding the lease, indicating whether such assertions are correct and the reasons therefore.

ANSWERS:

1. With either an assumption or a sublet, Fine will still be liable on the lease. This liability is based on the fact that Fine is still in privity of contract with Muni Bank. In order for Fine to be released, under the facts given, Fine needs a novation. The novation would substitute Bean for Fine. However, the novation requires a writing under the Statute of Frauds.

2. Anti-assignment clauses are valid and enforceable by the banks. During the high interest rates of the late 70s and early 80s, banks enforced these clauses to prevent the transfer of low rate mortgages. Courts have held that anti-assignment clauses do not constitute an alienation of property. However, Fine is correct that he has the right to sublet. If the lease is silent on the sublet, then Fine may sublet despite the anti-assignment clause. But, the sublet will not release him from his contractual duties.

MAY, 1987 NUMBER 4
LESSOR/LESSEE RIGHTS

Issues Tested:

I. Fixtures

A distinction exists between real and personal property. This distinction has been tested in the area of the lease. With the termination of a lease, the tenant/lessee can remove personal property. The landlord is entitled to the real property, but there is an unique problem with a fixture.

Personal property that becomes part of the real property is considered real property. The intent is the key. If the personal property is intended to be permanently affixed to the real property, then the item is a fixture. If the property is now a fixture, the tenant cannot remove it. In some jurisdictions, the law states that, if the fixture can be removed without damage to the real property, it remains removable as personal property. A ceiling fan is just such an example.

However, there is an exception to the exception. If the fixture is considered to be a trade fixture, then the lessee may remove it. An example could be a pizza oven. The oven is a fixture, since it is permanently attached to the real property. But as a fixture used in a trade or business, it may be removed by the lessee.

MAY, 1991 NUMBER 4
TRANSFER OF PROPERTY AT DEATH

Issues Tested:

    I.   Tenancy in Common
    II.   Insurable Interest
    III. Proceeds

There is no doubt that the AICPA will test on tenancy in common. The candidate must know that a tenant in common can alienate his/her interest in his/her will. The joint tenant cannot. A tenant in common has an insurable interest in property. If an insurance company consents to the assignment of insurance to a tenant in common, then the tenant is entitled to the proceeds of the insurance. It would seem disingenuous to allow the tenant in common to pay on the policy without the right to proceeds.

LONG OBJECTIVE FORMAT QUESTIONS
MAY, 1992 NUMBER 2
MORTGAGE PRIORITY

Issues Tested:

    I.   Recording Acts
    II. Foreclosure Proceeds

The candidate must know the recording acts. The AICPA will probably test on the NOTICE-RACE statute. In this case a bank will have priority over subsequent recording parties if the bank recorded first and recorded without knowledge of the earlier conveyances. It is important to note that the failure to record properly under the state's recording statutes does not change the relationship between the mortgagor and the mortgagee.

This priority is very important since the mortgage which has priority is satisfied in full before the proceeds are applied to lower priority interests. There is no pro-rata distribution, and the mortgagee is still liable for the deficiency. In mortgage foreclosure, be sure to mention the mortgagee's equitable and statutory rights of redemption. However, these rights probably do not apply, since then the AICPA could not ask about proceeds at foreclosure.

Remember, a grantee who takes the property subject to the mortgage does not assume personal liability. This grantee is not in privity of contract with the mortgagee, nor is he/she in privity of estate with the grantor.

LONG OBJECTIVE QUESTIONS
NOVEMBER, 1993 NUMBER 2
DEEDS AND MORTGAGE PRIORITY

Issues Tested:

    I.   Quitclaim Deed
    II.   General Warranty Deed
    III. Title Insurance
    IV. Priority
    V.   Co-Insurance

A quitclaim deed only transfers the interest the grantor has. If the grantor has no interest in the property, then the grantee/transferor has nothing. The best protection for the grantee is to demand a general warranty deed. A general warranty deed includes the covenant:

1. Seisin (the grantor has title)
2. The right to convey
3. No encumbrances
4. Quiet enjoyment (no one with superior title will disturb grantee's title)
5. Further assurances (grantor will perform in order to protect grantee's title)

Title insurance protects the buyer of the policy of defects in the title not discovered in the title examination. If there is a defect, the insurance company will pay the damages.

In mortgage foreclosure the priorities are normally determined by the priority under the recording act of that state. Foreclosure will remove all interests junior to the mortgage being foreclosed. The candidate should know that the foreclosure will not affect any senior interest.

INSURANCE

Insurance is lightly tested on the CPA Exam. In addition, this section is more predictable. The candidate should expect a question concerning an insurable interest. However, the candidate should be more prepared for a question (multiple choice or essay) on coinsurance. In fact, the candidate should commit the formula to memory.

I. Insurable Interest

This is a legal or equitable interest where the insured will suffer a loss (pecuniary) with the destruction of the insurance contract's subject matter, or receive a benefit for its preservation.

    A. Life

        1. The insured must have an insurable interest at the time the contract is made (a.k.a. when the policy is obtained). (T)

    B. Property

    The CPA Exam tests more extensively in this area.

        1. Insurable interest in property must be present at the time the loss occurs. (TTT)

May 1983 #36

The insurable interest in property

    a. can be waived by consent of the parties.
    b. is subject to the incontestability clause.

> c. **must be present at the time the loss occurs.**
> d. is only available to owners, occupiers, or users of the property.
>
> CHAPTER 52   SECTION 1   PAGES 931-932

2. Others, besides the owner, may also have an insurable interest in property. (TTT)

3. A corporate retailer has an insurable interest their inventory and a partner has an insurable interest in partnership property. (T)

C. Buyer of Goods (also study under Sales-Article 2 of the UCC)

A buyer of goods has an insurable interest in goods when the goods have been <u>identified</u> as part of the contract. (TT)

> November 1986 # 59
>
> The earliest time a purchaser of existing goods will acquire an insurable interest in those goods is when
>
> a. the purchaser obtains possession.
> b. title passes to the purchaser.
> c. performance of the contract has been completed or substantially completed.
> d. **the goods are identified to the contract.**
>
> CHAPTER 22   SECTION 1   PAGE 371

D. Seller of the Goods

The seller has an insurable interest until he/she receives the purchase price. (T) Therefore, the seller can still have an insurable interest even after sale! This is because the buyer might not have paid the full purchase price at the time of the sale, and the seller has a "secured interest" in the goods. (See Secured Transaction, UCC Article 9.)

II. Contract Issues

A. Conditions Precedent

An insurer's duty to pay under an insurance contract (policy) is not present unless the condition precedent happens. A condition precedent tells the insurer when his/her duty to pay begins. (TTT) An example would be insurable interest. (See also Common Law Contracts)

B. Auto Insurance

There are several tested subjects in this area.

1. The insurance company must come and defend the policyholder. (T)

2. After the insurance company pays the insured's loss, the insurer is subrogated to the claims of the insured. In other words, the insurer "steps in the shoes" of the insured. (T)

3. Under the concept of subrogation, the insurer has a legal action for the amount of damages it paid. (T) The amount would be the full damage minus the insured's deductible.

II. Coinsurance

There most likely will be a question is this area. Coinsurance is for a <u>partial</u> <u>loss</u> only. (WTTT) Coinsurance encourages the insured to maintain a certain amount of insurance on his/her property in relation to the property's "fair market value." If not, then the insured must proportionally bear the loss. (WT) The student should also be prepared to calculate coinsurance with two insurance companies. (T)

May 1985 # 59

The coinsurance clause with regard to property insurance

a. prohibits the insured from obtaining an amount of insurance which would be less than the coinsurance percentage multiplied by the fair market value of the property.
b. encourages the insured to be more careful in preventing losses since the insured is always at least partially at risk when a loss occurs.
c. permits the insured to receive an amount in excess of the policy amount when there has been a total loss and the insured carried the clause.

196   Business Law and the CPA Exam

> d. will result in the insured sharing in partial losses when the insured has failed to carry the required coverage under the coinsurance clause.
>
> CHAPTER 52   SECTION 2   PAGE 936

A. The candidate should commit the following formula to memory:

$$\frac{\text{Amount of Insurance Carried}}{\text{Coinsurance \% } \times \text{ Fair Market Value (Replacement Value)}} \times \underline{\text{Actual}} \text{ Loss} = \text{Amount of Recovery}$$

> May 1990 # 59
>
> Lawfo Corp. maintains a $200,000 standard fire insurance policy on one of its warehouses. The policy includes an 80% coinsurance clause. At the time the warehouse was originally insured, its value was $250,000. The warehouse now has a value of $300,000. If the warehouse sustains $30,000 of fire damage, Lawfo's insurance recovery will be a maximum of
>
> a. $20,000.
> b. $24,000.
> **c. $25,000.**
> d. $30,000.
>
> CHAPTER 52   SECTION 1   PAGE 936

ESSAY QUESTIONS

NOVEMBER, 1982 NUMBER 5a
PARTIAL LOSS ON A BUILDING

Issues Tested:

I.   Coinsurance
II. Allocation

While auditing the financial statements of Jackson Corporation for the year ended December 31, 1981, Harvey Draper, CPA, desired to verify the balance in the insurance claims receivable account. Draper obtained the following information.

On November 3, 1981, Jackson's Parksdale plant was damaged by fire. The fire caused $200,000 damages to the plant, which was purchased in 1970 for $600,000. When the plant was purchased, Jackson obtained a loan secured by a mortgage from Second National Bank of Parksdale. At the time of the fire, the loan balance, including accrued interest, was $106,000. The plant was insured against fire with Eagle Insurance Company. The policy contained a "standard mortgage" clause and an 80% coinsurance clause. The face value of the policy was $600,000, and the value of the plant was $1,000,000 at the time of the fire.

On December 10, 1981, Jackson's Yuma warehouse was totally destroyed by fire. The warehouse was acquired in 1960 for $300,000. At the time of the fire, the warehouse was unencumbered by any mortgage; it was insured against fire with Eagle for $300,000, and it had a value of $500,000. The policy contained an 80% coinsurance clause.

On December 26, 1982, Jackson's Rye City garage was damaged by fire. At the time of the fire, the garage had a value of $250,000 and was unencumbered by any mortgage. The fire caused $60,000 damage to the garage, which was constructed in 1965 at a cost of $50,000. In 1957, Jackson expanded the capacity of the garage at an additional cost of $50,000 with Eagle, and this policy was still in force on the fire date. When the garage was expanded in 1975, Jackson obtained $100,000 of additional fire insurance coverage from Queen Insurance Company. Each policy contains an 80% coinsurance clause and a standard pro rata clause.

REQUIRED

Answer the following, setting forth reasons for any conclusions stated.

1. How much of the fire loss relating to the Parksdale plant will be recovered from Eagle?

2. How will such recovery be distributed between Second National and Jackson?

3. How much of the fire loss relating to the Yuma warehouse will be recovered from Eagle?

4. What portion of the amount recoverable in connection with Rye City garage loss will Queen be obligated to pay?

SOLUTION

The candidate should memorize the following formula for the essay and multiple choice questions.

$$\frac{\text{Amount of Insurance Carried}}{\text{Fair Market Value of the Property} \times \text{Coinsurance Percent}} \times \text{Amount of Partial Loss} = \text{Recovery}$$

1. $$\frac{\$600,000}{\$1,000,000 \times 80\%} \times \$200,000 = \$150,000$$

2. Of this $150,000 the bank receives the first $106,000, and Jackson Corporation would receive the balance.

3. The Yuma warehouse was <u>totally</u> destroyed. The coinsurance only applies with a <u>partial</u> loss. So Jackson would receive the face value of the policy.

4. $$\frac{\$50,000 + \$100,000}{\$250,000 \times 80\%} \times \$60,00 = \$45,000$$

5. $$\frac{\$100,000}{\$50,000 + \$100,000} \times \$45,000 = \$30,000$$

NOVEMBER, 1988 NUMBER 2
FIRE AND CASUALTY INSURANCE

Issues Tested:

   I.   Contract Modification and Statute of Frauds
   II. Insurable Interest
   III. Coinsurance
   IV. Payment Percentage

Although contract modification is normally tested in Common Law Contracts, the candidate should be prepared to answer contract questions in other sections. First, if a contract is modified, then new consideration is needed. Next, if the modification is within the Statute of Frauds, then a writing or memo is required.

Insurable interest in property must exist at the time the loss occurs, not when the policy is obtained.

The insurable interest can be a monetary loss.

For coinsurance, see the multiple choice questions or the essay question of November, 1982. As with the November, 1982, essay question, an insurance company is only liable for its portion of loss among all insurance carriers.

MAY, 1991 NUMBER 4
FIRE AND CASUALTY

Issues Tested:

    I.   Coinsurance
    II. Insurable Interest
    III. Recording Acts
    IV. Proceeds of Contingent Beneficiaries
    V. Implied Warranty of Habitability
    VI. Constructive Eviction

Again the candidate should be prepared for coinsurance and other related insurance topics. However, just as with contract law, the AICPA will use insurance law to test other areas.

The tenant has the modern theory of the implied warranty of habitability. In the past, the tenant received only the right to possess the property. Today, not only must the landlord deliver possession, but in habitable form. Violation to comply with building or health codes is a breach of the lease.

In addition, if the property is not in habitable condition, the tenant might also claim constructive eviction. Here, the landlord has made the tenancy so untenable that it is as if the landlord has evicted the tenant. No heat or no water would be an example. The tenant, in most jurisdictions, must vacate the property to make a claim of constructive eviction. Also, a tenant can be partially evicted from his/her property.

LONG OBJECTIVE QUESTIONS
NOVEMBER, 1993 NUMBER 2
RESIDENCE FIRE

    Issues Tested:

        I.   Coinsurance
        II. Property Law

LONG OBJECTIVE QUESTIONS
MAY, 1994 NUMBER 3b

FACTORY FIRE

Issues Tested:

I. Insurable Interest in Property
II. Coinsurance
III. Coinsurance with multiple carriers

ESTATES AND TRUSTS

I. Estates

The AICPA tests much more heavily on Trusts than Estates (Wills).

A. Probate estates are liable for the debts of the testator. (T) These rules are much more complex than this general rule, yet the CPA Exam tests no further.

B. The personal representative (a.k.a. "executor" or "administrator") is a fiduciary who files accounts with the probate court and holds legal title to the estate property. (T)

C. Per Capita vs Per Stirpes

This is the hardest section in Estates. It is beyond the scope of this supplement to reteach this subject. In a PER STIRPES distribution the first level after the testator takes its distribution, and all the remaining heirs take through their bloodlines. Be forewarned that a PER CAPITA distribution looks for the generational level with the first live heir, and then the distribution takes per stirpes. (T)

November 1992 # 9

A descendant's will provided that the estate was to be divided among the decedent's issue, per capita and not per stirpes. If there are two surviving children and three grandchildren who are children of a predeceased child at the time the will is probated, how will the estate be divided?

   a.   1/2 to each surviving child.
   b.   1/3 to each surviving child and 1/9 to each grandchild.
   c.   1/4 to each surviving child and 1/6 to each grandchild.
   d.   1/5 to each surviving child and grandchild.

CHAPTER 53   SECTION 2   PAGES 955-957

202   Business Law and the CPA Exam

II. Trusts

　　A. Formation or the Elements of a Trust

　　　　1. Identifiable Beneficiaries (A trust could fail if the sole beneficiary is also the sole remainderman and the sole trustee.) (T)

　　　　2. A funded trust (res or corpus or property) (T)

　　　　3. Purpose

　　　　　　If the purpose of a trust is no longer valid, the trustee can ask the court to continue the trust with a purpose that is "as near as" the original purpose. This is called "Cy Pres." (T)

　　　　4. Settlor/grantor/trustor with capacity.

　　　　5. The AICPA exam will expect the candidate to know that a trust is still valid even if a successor trustee is not named. (T) In fact, in many states a trust will not fail for the lack of an initial trustee (a court can always appoint one later).

November 1991 # 18

Which of the following is **not** necessary to create an express trust?

　　a. A trust corpus.
　　b. A successor trustee.
　　c. A valid trust purpose.
　　d. A beneficiary.

CHAPTER 53　　SECTION 3　　PAGE 957

　　B. Types of Trusts

　　　　1. Inter Vivos

　　　　　　An expressed trust created during the lifetime of the Settlor. (T)

　　　　2. Testamentary

An expressed trust which takes effect at the death of the settlor. (TT) Also, the settlor has fiduciary duties and can reserve the right to make the trust revocable. (T)

3. Resulting Trust

A trust inferred by law to carry out the purpose of the settlor. A resulting trust and the doctrine of "cy pres" are not the same legal concept. (T)

4. Spendthrift

A Spendthrift Trust provides for the maintenance of the beneficiary and prevents the beneficiary from transferring his/her beneficial interest in the trust. (T)

5. Charitable Trusts and The Rule Against Perpetuities

The CPA Exam will not test on the easy and obvious definition of a CHARITABLE TRUST. The candidate must know, however, the innocuous legal doctrine known as the "Rule Against Perpetuities" (RAP). Still, the AICPA will not test on the more difficult elements of the rule. (No one understands RAP completely!) Yet, the candidate should know that charitable trusts are not subject to RAP! (WT) Under RAP an interest in property (e.g. a future interest in a trust) must vest, if at all, not later than a life in being plus 21 years at the creation of the interest. (WT) This rule does NOT apply to future interests in the grantor.

C. Trustee Duties

1. A Trustee is a Fiduciary.

a. The trustee is guided by the "Prudent Trustee Rule." He/she must invest the trust money in order to provide a safe return. If a trustee is negligent in his/her duties, then he/she violates the "Prudent Trustee Rule" (WTT) (but see footnote 6 on page 961)

b. A Trustee must be loyal to the trust. (T)

May 1982 #55

Assuming that a given trust is silent on the point, the trustee has certain rights and duties as a matter of law. The trustee

- a. has a fiduciary duty to the trust but <u>not</u> to the beneficiaries.
- b. is <u>not</u> entitled to commissions unless so provided.
- c. can elect to terminate the trust as long as the beneficiaries unanimously concur.
- **d. must act in a competent, nonnegligent manner, or he/she may face removal.**

CHAPTER N/A   SECTION N/A   PAGE N/A

D. Trustee Powers

1. The trustee has expressed and implied powers. (WT)

2. The trustee has the power to delegate administrative duties (e.g. tax returns). (WT)

3. The trustee does need beneficiary approval for major investment changes. (WT) Of course, the trustee is subject to the "Prudent Trustee Rule."

E. Termination of a Trust

1. By Time

If the trust is only for a specific time period, the trust will terminate with the expiration of time. (T)

November 1990 # 20

A trust will be terminated if

- a. a beneficiary becomes incompetent.
- b. the trustee dies.
- c. the grantor dies.
- **d. the trust terms expires.**

CHAPTER 53   SECTION 3   PAGE 962

2. By Operation of Law (e.g. illegality) (WT)

3. Merger

    In a trust the trustee has legal title to trust property, while the beneficiary has beneficial title. If the two titles ever "merge" in the hands of one person the trust could terminate (e.g. the sole beneficiary becomes the sole trustee). (WT)

4. Another way a trust terminates, or in this case fails, is if the transfer of property is a gift. A gift is irrevocable, while a trust may be revocable. (WT)

5. If an irrevocable trust does not provide a method of termination, then a court has the power to terminate the trust. (WT) The remaindermen will receive the assets of a terminated trust. (WT)

F. Tax

1. The trust is a separate legal entity for tax purposes. (WT)

2. A testamentary trust can avoid federal estate taxes if the trust funds are transferred to the surviving spouse. This is called the Unlimited Marital Deduction. (WT)

G. Allocation between Income Beneficiaries and Principal Beneficiaries

The trustee must be impartial in his/her treatment of the these two beneficiaries, yet there are rules on how to allocate certain trust costs. The text does not explore all allocations, but here they will be differentiated.

1. Principal

    a. Mortgage principal payments (WTT)

    b. Extraordinary matters and improvements (T)

    c. Sale of bonds and trust property (WT)

    d. Stock dividends (WT)

    e. Settlement of trust property (WT)

    f. Sidewalk assessments (WTT)

g. Insurance settlements (WT)

   1) Insurance premiums (WT)

h. One contract (WT)

i. Sale of the sole trust property (WT)

2. Income

   a. Depreciation (WT)

   b. Forfeited deposits (WT)

   c. Mortgage interest (WTT)

   d. Rents (TT)

   e. CD and bond interest (WT)

   f. Royalties (WT)

   g. Cash dividends (WT)

   h. Income (WT)

November 1981 #51

The Martin Trust consisted primarily of various income-producing real estate properties. During the year, the trustee incurred various charges. Among the charges were the following: depreciation, principal payments on various mortgages, and a street assessment. Which of the following would be a proper allocation of these items?

   a. All to income, except the street assessment.
   b. All are to be allocated equally between principal and income.
   c. All to principal.
   d. All to principal, except depreciation.

CHAPTER 53   SECTION 3   PAGE 962

ESSAY QUESTIONS

The CPA Exam will test on trusts before it concentrates on estates. In addition, the candidate should prepare for an estate tax problem.

MAY, 1984 NUMBER 4
CREATION AND MANAGEMENT OF A TRUST

Tested Issues:

I. Elements
II. Trustee
III. Termination
IV. Trust Interest

The candidate should know the elements of trust for the essay, as well as the multiple choice section. The elements include:

1. A settlor with capacity
2. Res (property)
3. Purpose
4. Intent
5. Identifiable Beneficiaries

A trustee or a successor trustee is not a requirement. The trust will not fail for a lack of a trustee, since the court can appoint one. The settlor cannot be the sole beneficiary and the sole trustee. But the sole beneficiary can be a co-trustee.

In this essay question, the AICPA tested on trustee duties and not powers. The trustee possesses legal title to trust property, while the beneficiaries retain beneficiary title. The trustee has the duty to preserve the trust property. Just as the director of a corporation has the defense of the Business Judgment Rule for his/her negligence, the trustee has the Prudent Trustee Rule. The trustee is not the guarantor of high investment returns, yet the trustee is expected to put trust assets in incoming producing instruments. The trust must be productive.

There are several ways to terminate a trust. However, the least obvious is a merger. If legal title and beneficiary title ever come together, the trust terminates. Consequently, if the sole beneficiary ever becomes the sole trustee, then trust terminates due to merger of title.

In the trust essay question, the AICPA tests the candidate on certain property issues. The candidate should be able to distinguish among tenancy by the entirety, a tenancy in common, and joint tenancy. Only a few states recognize the holding of property by a married couple in tenancy by the entirety. In this case the husband and the wife each own all of the property held by the married couple. Therefore, neither party can alienate the other spouse's interest without consent.

Tenancy in common is a method of holding property where each tenant in common owns a divided portion of a whole. The tenant in common can alienate the property by will, sale, or gift.

Joint tenancy is a holding of property where each joint tenant owns an undivided, equal portion of a whole. The joint tenant cannot alienate his/her interest by will. His/her interest, at death, is transferred to the surviving joint tenants. A joint tenant can sell his/her interest. The transferee is not a joint tenant, but a tenant in common. The surviving joint tenants do remain as joint tenant with the surviving joint tenants.

MAY, 1987 NUMBER 5
ALLOCATION PRINCIPAL AND INTEREST IN AN INTER VIVOS TRUST

Issues Tested:

I. Elements of Trust
II. Allocation of Principal and Interest

An inter vivos trust is a trust created and administered during the settlor's lifetime. The special difference in the elements of the inter vivos trust is that the settlor must show the present intent to transfer interest (res/property). An excellent example of a inter vivos trust is the new and popular revocable "living trust." The living trust would be an excellent forum for future trust test questions.

The trustee must treat the beneficiaries equally and fairly. This fiduciary duty becomes more complicated with principal and income beneficiaries. If the trust is silent on the allocation of expenses and income, the trust should follow special common law or statutory rules. The principal beneficiaries' (a.k.a. remaindermen) interest is in the res or the corpus of the trust. The income beneficiaries are entitled to the income of trust, minus certain expenses. The sale of stock, mortgage principal payment, and sidewalk assessments are allocated to the principal beneficiaries, while rental income, mortgage interest payments, building management fees, and depreciation are allocated to the income beneficiaries.

NOVEMBER, 1989 NUMBER 2
THE TRANSFER AND LIABILITY OF LAND/SPENDTHRIFT TRUSTS

Issues Tested:

I. Loan Assumption
II. Due on Sale Clause
III. Tenants in Common

IV. Spendthrift Trust
V. Trust Termination

If a mortgage note is silent as to the assumption of the note, then the note would be assumable. The typical restriction would be a "due on sale" clause. Here if the restriction is not on the note, then the note is assumable. If the note is assumable, then the transferee of the property is liable on the note. The transferor of the property remains liable on the note.

The AICPA rarely tests on estates in the essay section. But a typical question it would ask would be the transferability of property at death. If property is owned in joint tenancy, the property is automatically transferred to the surviving joint tenants. Joint tenancy avoids probate. If the parties are tenants in common, then the tenant in common may alienate the property through his/her will.

A spendthrift trust is a trust used by the settlor to prevent the beneficiary's mismanagement. The settlor prevents the beneficiary from transferring trust income or principal. In fact, the settlor can protect the beneficiary's interest from the beneficiary's creditor. However the law in most states will not let the settlor avoid his/her own creditors with a spendthrift trust/clause.

As stated previously, there are several methods to terminate a trust. If the trustees can no longer serve the trust purpose, then the trust may fail. However the court can use "cy pres" in order to keep the trust from failing. The courts disdain forfeiture and will find a trust purpose that is "as near as" the original purpose. Merger of the equitable and beneficial title can also terminate the trust.

Finally, if all beneficiaries agree, the trust can terminate. However, the court could appoint a guardian/conservator who will protect the interest of minor or unborn children. Guardians/conservators rarely allow the termination of the trust if the termination could injure the future interests of the children. Also, if all beneficiaries agree to terminate a spendthrift trust, this termination would defeat the purpose of the trust. The court should not grant the beneficiaries such a request.

NOVEMBER, 1993 NUMBER 3
THE MANAGEMENT OF A SPENDTHRIFT TRUST

Issues Tested:

I. Termination
II. Trustee Duties

A spendthrift trust is a type of trust that places trust property with instructions not to let the imprudent beneficiary access. The more practical view is that a trust contains a spendthrift <u>clause</u>

that restricts the beneficiary's creditors from executing judgment on the beneficiary's interest.

Of course, one method of terminating a trust is by an agreement of all the beneficiaries. However, with a spendthrift trust, or a trust with a spendthrift clause, the purpose of the trust would be defeated if the beneficiaries could exercise such control. The judge in this case would not let the trust terminate.

While it would be proper for a trustee to challenge the beneficiaries in the above example, the trustee still owes fiduciary duties to the beneficiaries. The trustee would breach this duty of trust by commingling the trustee's own assets with those of the trust. In addition, the trustee cannot borrow trust funds.

NOVEMBER, 1994 NUMBER 4
INTER VIVOS SPENDTHRIFT TRUST

Issues Tested:

    I.   Requirements of a valid inter vivos spendthrift trust
    II.   Allocation of principal and income
    III. Termination of a trust

LONG OBJECTIVE QUESTIONS
NOVEMBER, 1995 NUMBER 2b
TESTAMENTARY TRUST ADMINISTRATION

Issues Tested:

    I.   Rule Against Perpetuities
    II.   Distribution to Principal and Income Beneficiaries
    III. Trust Termination
    IV. Trustee's Fiduciary Duties

ACCOUNTANT LIABILITY

This section of the CPA Exam is comprehensive in nature. The candidate must be familiar with the many areas of the exam. You should know Tort Law (for fraud), Contract Law, and Securities Regulation. Before studying Accountant Liability, you must be comfortable with the above areas.

I. Common Law Liability to Clients

   A. Contract Law

   1. If an accountant does not perform the services as promised, the accountant can be liable for breach of contract. (TT)

   2. An accountant can be liable for his own breach, but not for the fraud of his client. (T)

   3. There is no strict liability standard in contract. This standard belongs in tort law. (T)

   4. Accountants use engagement letters to delineate rights and duties between themselves and their clients. This sounds like contract law. However, it would be against public policy to use the engagement letter to release the accountant from all tort liability. (T)

II. Common Law Tort Liability to Clients

   A. Negligence (elements of) (TTT)

   The candidate must know the elements of the tort of negligence.

   1. Duty

   2. Breach of Duty

212   Business Law and the CPA Exam

3. Causation

   a. Real Cause ("but for" test), and

   b. Proximate Cause (foreseeability test)

4. Damages (monetary)

B. Testable Issues in Negligence

1. An accountant will meet his/her duty to his/her client, if the accountant uses the average degree of learning, skill, care, knowledge and judgement generally accepted by the members of the profession. (TT)

2. The failure to GAAP or GAAS is *prima facie* proof of negligence. (TT)

November 1983 #3

Gleam is contemplating a common law action against Moore & Co., CPAs, based upon fraud. Gleam loaned money to Lilly & Company relying upon Lilly's financial statements which were audited by Moore. Gleams's action will fail if

a. Gleam shows only that Moore failed to meticulously follow GAAP.
b. Moore can establish that it fully complied with the Statute of Frauds.
c. The alleged fraud was in part committed by oral misrepresentations and Moore pleads the parol evidence rule.
d. Gleam is not a third party beneficiary in light of the absence of privity.

CHAPTER 54   SECTION 1   PAGES 970-974

---

3. However, proof of GAAP or GAAS is not a defense to claim of negligence. (TT)

November 1983 #4

In an action for negligence against a CPA, the "custom of the profession" standard is used at least to some extent in determining whether the CPA is negligent. Which of the following statements describes how this standard is applied?

> a. If the CPA proves he literally followed GAAP and GAAS, it will be conclusively presumed that the CPA was <u>not</u> negligent.
> b. The ""custom of the profession" argument may only be raised by the defendant.
> c. **Despite a CPAs adherence to the custom of the profession, negligence may nevertheless be present.**
> d. Failure to satisfy the custom of the profession is equivalent to gross negligence.
>
> CHAPTER 54   SECTION 1   PAGES 970-971

4. There is no negligence for failure to discover another's fraud. However, if the accountant's <u>own</u> negligence precluded the discovery of that fraud or the correction of an error, then the accountant is negligent. (TT)

5. An honest error in judgment is <u>not</u> negligence. (TT)

6. Defenses (TT)

   a. Lack of negligence .

   b. Lack of proximate cause (e.g. the client lost money, but the accountant's error [breach of duty] did not cause the loss).

   c. Client's own negligence or fraud.

7. In an unaudited financial statement, the accountant has a lesser standard of care (duty). But an accountant can still be liable for failure to use standard accounting practices and to give proper disclosure of potential fraud. (T)

8. An accountant has a duty to notify the client of known internal control weaknesses. (WT)

C. Intentional Tort (Fraud)

   1. Actual Fraud (TTT)

      a. MISREPRESENTATION of a MATERIAL fact

      b. Knowledge or belief of the accountant that the statement is false

(SCIENTER) (T)

c. INTENT to deceive

d. JUSTIFIABLE RELIANCE on the part of the client. This element is also required for negligent misrepresentation (WT)

e. DAMAGES

May 1981 #6

If a CPA firm is being sued for common law fraud by a third party based upon materially false financial statements, which of the following is the best defense which the accountants could assert?

a. Lack of privity.
b. Lack of reliance.
c. A disclaimer contained in the engagement letter.
d. Contributory negligence on the part of the client.

CHAPTER 54   SECTION 1   PAGES 973-974

---

2. Constructive Fraud

The accountant can be liable for CONSTRUCTIVE FRAUD, if the accountant is grossly negligent in the performance of his duties. For instance, the accountant had no knowledge that the statement is false, but performed his duties with reckless disregard for the truth. (TT)

3. Defenses

a. Contract defenses (lack of consideration, duress, etc.) are not defenses in tort (negligence or fraud). (T)

b. Also, do not confuse negligence defenses (lack of proximate cause or contributory negligence) with fraud defenses. (T)

c. For fraud defenses see the above elements. If one element is missing, then there is no fraud. (T)

III. Liability to Third Parties

   A. Common Law Contract Liability

   There can be no contract liability to third parties just by definition. A third party is a party who does not have a contract with the accountant. This is also called the lack of privity.

   B. Tort Liability in Negligence to Third Parties

   The AICPA rarely, if at all, tests in the area of common law accountant fraud liability to third parties.

   1. The *Ultramares* Test

   Traditionally, accountants owe a duty of care only to those with whom they are in privity of contract. *Ultramares* holds that the accountant is liable to those with whom the accountant is in privity or to those in a relationship that is "so close as to approach that of privity." This is tough standard for a third party to meet. (TTT)

November 1991 #4

Hark, CPA, failed to follow generally accepted auditing standards when auditing Long Corporation's financial statements. Long's management had told Hark that the audited statements would be submitted to several banks to obtain financing. Relying on the statements, Third Bank gave Long a loan. In a jurisdiction applying the *Ultramares* decision, if Third sues Hark, Hark will

   a. win because there was no privity of contract between Hark and Third.
   b. lose because Hark knew that banks would be relying on the financial statements.
   c. win because Third was contributorily negligent in granting the loan.
   d. lose because Hark was negligent in performing the audit.

CHAPTER 54   SECTION 2   PAGE 975

---

   2. The Restatement of Torts (Second) Test

   The RESTATEMENT relaxes the *Ultramares* Test. In this case the accountant liability extends not only to those the accountant is in privity, but also to those who reasonably and foreseeably would rely on accountant's statements and audits. This is an easier standard for the third party to meet. (T)

3. State Variations

The law is this area is changing with no definitive uniform standard. Therefore, the AICPA will not test on the even more relaxed standards of certain states' case laws.

III. Federal Statutory Liability

A. Section 11 of the Securities Act of 1933

1. An accountant who prepares statements for the registration statement is liable for the misstatements and omissions of material facts. (TT)

November 1983 # 5

Lewis & Clark, CPAs, rendered an unqualified opinion on the financial statements of a company that sold common stock in a public offering subject to the Securities Act of 1933. Based on a false statement in the financial statements, Lewis & Clark are being sued by an investor who purchased shares of this public offering. Which of the following represents a viable defense?

a. The investor has not met the burden of proving fraud or negligence by Lewis & Clark.
b. The investor did not actually rely upon false statement.
c. **Detection of the false statement by Lewis & Clark occurred after their examination date.**
d. Only applies to preparers of individual tax returns.

CHAPTER 54   SECTION 4   PAGES 978-979

---

2. The purchaser/plaintiff only needs to show that he/she suffered a LOSS. (TT)

3. The purchaser/plaintiff does not have to show PRIVITY or RELIANCE. (TT) The candidate should remember reliance, important under the 1934 Act, is an element of fraud.

May 1993 # 5

To be successful in a civil action under Section 11 of the Securities Act of 1933 concerning liability for a misleading registration statement, the plaintiff must prove the

	Defendant's intent to deceive	Plaintiff's reliance on the registration statement
a.	No	Yes
b.	**No**	**No**
c.	Yes	No
d.	Yes	Yes

CHAPTER 54   SECTION 4   PAGES 978-979

4. Defenses to Section 11 of the 1933 Act

   a. The accountant used "due diligence." (TT)

   b. Other defenses resort to attacking the purchaser/plaintiff's case. (TT)

      1) The purchaser/plaintiff knew of the misstatement or omission.

      2) The misstatements or omissions were not material.

      3) There were no misstatements or omissions in the registration statement, or there was no connection between the these errors and the loss.

   c. The accountant used GAAP. (T)

May 1981 # 3

Major, Minor & Sharpe, CPAs, are the auditors of MacLain Industries. In connection with the public offering of $10 million of MacLain securities, Major expressed an unqualified opinion as to the financial statements. Subsequent to the offering, certain misstatements and omissions were revealed. Major has been sued by the purchasers of the stock offered pursuant to the registration statement which included the financial statements audited by Major. In the ensuing lawsuit by the MacLain investors, Major will be able to avoid liability if

    a.   the errors and omissions were caused primarily by MacLain.
    b.   it can be shown that at least some of the investors did <u>not</u> actually read the audited financial statements.
    c.   it can prove due diligence in the audit of the financial statements of MacLain.
    d.   MacLain had expressly assumed any liability in connection with the public offering.

CHAPTER 54   SECTION 4   PAGES 978-979

        The purchaser/plaintiff can recover the difference between the amount paid and the value of the security, at the time of disposal, before the suit, or at the time of the suit. (T)

    5.   Section 11 has a 3-year statute of limitation. (T)

B.   Section 18 of the Securities Exchange Act of 1934 (Think fraud!)

    1.   An accountant is liable for false and/or misleading statements of material facts made in the documents filed with the SEC. (TT) The candidate should not confuse this section with Section 11 of the 1933 Act. The candidate should remember that this section looks more like fraud.

    2.   Defenses to a Section 18 suit; as stated above, the defenses will look more like fraud defenses.

        a.   Good faith (TT)

        b.   Lack of the intent to deceive (TT)

C.   Section 10(b) and SEC Rule 10b-5

    1.   Section 10(b) imposes liability on those who use any manipulative or deceptive devise in connection with the sale or purchase of securities (T)

    2.   These anti-fraud provisions also make trading on inside information actionable. (T)

3. Rule 10b-5 also makes it unlawful for persons who trade securities in interstate commerce to do the following: (T)

   a. Employ any devise, scheme or artifice to defraud.

   b. Make any untrue statement of a material fact or omit to state a material fact necessary to make the statements asserted, made in light of the circumstances, not misleading.

   c. Engage in any act, practice, or course of business which operates or would operate as a fraud or deceit upon any person.

May 1992 #4

Dart Corporation engaged Jay Associates, CPAs, to assist in a public stock offering. Jay audited Dart's financial statements and gave an unqualified opinion, despite knowing that the financial statements contained misstatements. Jay's opinion was included in Dart's registration statement. Larson purchased shares in the offering and suffered a loss when the stock declined in value after the misstatements became known.

In a suit against Jay under the anti-fraud provisions of Section 10(b) and Rule 10b-5 of the Securities and Exchange Act of 1934, Larson must prove the following except

a. Larson was an intended user of the false registration statement.
b. Larson relied on the false registration statement.
c. the transaction involved some form of interstate commerce.
d. Jay acted with intentional disregard of the truth.

CHAPTER 54   SECTION 4   PAGE 980

---

4. The candidate must remember this is a fraud standard; therefore privity is not a necessary element. (T)

5. For an individual plaintiff (purchaser or seller) to sue an accountant on the antifraud provisions, the third party/plaintiff must establish:

   a. The statement or omission was material.

b. The accountant intended to deceive or defraud others.

c. The third party/plaintiff relied on the misrepresentations.

d. The purchaser or seller has damages (e.g. a loss).

e. An accountant will be liable under Section 10(b) if they acted without good faith. (T)

IV. Working Papers and Accountant-Client Privilege

   A. Working Papers

   1. Absent an agreement with the client, the working papers are the accountant's work product and property. (T)

   2. The accountant has a duty not to disclose the contents of the working papers, except under the following conditions: (T)

      a. Client sues the accountant.

      b. Client provides permission.

      c. A court orders, with a subpoena, the accountant. (T)

      d. A CPA (GAAP/GAAS) review board orders the accountant, if the state has a accountant-client privilege statute.

   3. The accountant can not transfer the working papers, without the consent of the client. (T) In essence, the accountant has no common law property right to his own client.

   B. Privileged Communication (see above IV,A,2,d)

   While many professions, by common law or statute, have client-professional privilege, the common law does not provide the accountant the same privilege. However, several states (e.g. Missouri) do provide this privilege by statute. (T) The candidate should be aware that if the AICPA ever tests more extensively in this area, that this privilege is the client's right and not the accountant's shield! The AICPA could test on this issue in the Ethics Section. The candidate should know that the profession's ethic would demand that the accountant, absent court order, not reveal client communications.

May 1981 #2

The CPA firm of Knox & Knox has been subpoenaed to testify and produce its correspondence and workpapers in connection with a lawsuit brought by a third party against one of their clients. Knox considers the subpoenaed documents to be privileged communications and therefore seeks to avoid admission of such evidence in the lawsuit. Which of the following is correct?

a. Federal law recognizes such a privilege if the accountant is a Certified Public Accountant.
b. The privilege is available regarding the working papers since the CPA is deemed to own them.
c. The privileged communication rule as it applies to the CPA-client relationship is the same as that of attorney-client.
d. In the absence of a specific statutory provision, the law does not recognize the existence of the privileged communication rule between a CPA and his client.

CHAPTER 54   SECTION 6   PAGE 982-983

V. Tax Preparation

A. If a CPA does a tax return and charges a fee, then he must keep the return for three years or face a penalty. (WT)

B. IRC Section 6700 holds that any person who organizes (attorney) or aids in the organization (accountant) of an entity (partnership, corporation, etc.) and knowingly makes a false statement as to any material item, will be penalized to the greater of $1,000 or 20% of the gross income received. (WT)

C. If a tax preparer endorses or cashes his client's refund check, IRC Section 6695 imposes a penalty. (T)

November 1993 #9

Clark, a professional tax return preparer, prepared and signed a client's 1992 federal income tax return that resulted in a $600 refund. Which one of the following statements is correct with regard to an internal Revenue Code penalty Clark may be subject to for endorsing and cashing the client's refund check?

> a. **Clark will be subject to the penalty if Clark endorsed and cashed the check.**
> b. Clark may endorse and cash the check, without penalty, if Clark enrolled to practice before the Internal Revenue Service.
> c. Clark may not endorse and cash the check, without penalty, because the check is for more than $500.
> d. Clark may endorse and cash the check, without penalty, if the amount does not exceed Clark's fee for preparation of the return.
>
> CHAPTER 54   SECTION 5   PAGE 982

D. Section 6695 also extends liability for failing to furnish the taxpayer with a copy of the return, for failing to provide a tax ID numbers, or for failing to sign his client's return.

E. IRC Section 7206 makes the assisting of a false return a felony.

F. IRC Section 6694 imposes penalties on the tax preparer for the negligent or willful understatement of the client's tax bill. The accountant would not be liable if he used due diligence in the research of his client's tax liability. In fact, the accountant can avoid liability if the accountant relied in good faith in his client's assertions. (TT)

G. The tax preparer must inform the client of previous tax preparation errors. (T)

H. The IRS has comprehensive enforcement powers. These powers range from fines and injunctions to criminal prosection. (TT)

> May 1989 #3
>
> Tax preparers who aid and abet federal tax evasion are subject to
>
> | | Injunction to be prohibited from acting as tax preparers | General federal criminal prosecution |
> |---|---|---|
> | a. | No | No |
> | b. | Yes | No |
> | c. | No | Yes |

d.	Yes		Yes

CHAPTER 54   SECTION 5   PAGE 982

ESSAY QUESTIONS

The questions is this section are straightforward and predictable. You should have a full understanding of the elements of negligence and fraud. Also, you should study securities regulations and the variations of the *Ultramares* and the second restatements of torts on third-party liability.

MAY, 1986 NUMBER 2
ACCOUNTANT LIABILITY

Issues Tested:

   I.   Negligence
   II. Third Party Liability
   III. Fraud

The candidate must know the elements of the *prima facie* case of negligence. The failure to use GAAP/GAAS is *prima facie* proof of negligence. However, the use of GAAP/GAAS is not a complete defense.

The candidate should be familiar with all the third party liability theories. These theories include the third party beneficiary contract status and the *Ultramares* case.

Finally, the candidate should not confuse negligence with fraud. Fraud's special requirements include scienter, reliance and misrepresentation of a material fact.

MAY, 1987 NUMBER 3
ACCOUNTANT MALPRACTICE

Issues Tested:

   I.   Accountant-Client Privilege
   II. Negligence
   III. Third Party Liability
   IV. GAAP/GAAS Standards
   V.   Actual/Constructive Fraud

The candidate should know that the accountant-client privilege is not recognized under the common law. In fact, only a few states recognize the privilege by statute.

The difference between actual fraud and constructive fraud is that, with constructive fraud, the plaintiff does not have to show actual knowledge of the falsity, but reckless disregard for the truth.

MAY, 1988 NUMBER 5c
ENFORCEABLE AGREEMENTS AND ACCOUNTANT MALPRACTICE

Issues Tested:

    I.   Statute of Frauds
    II.   Covenants Not to Compete
    III. Unqualified Opinions

The AICPA will expect the candidate to know that contracts that take, by their own terms, longer than a year to perform will require a writing. Only full performance within the one year will take the contract out of the Statute of Frauds, and let the oral contract stand.

The restriction of one's livelihood is normally unenforceable as a restraint of trade. But courts will enforce a covenant not to compete, if the covenant is reasonable in the restrictions of time and distance. The covenant will appear in two fact patterns. The first is an employment contract, and the other will be with the sale of a business' goodwill.

Accountants still owe a duty to exercise due care with an unqualified opinion.

NOVEMBER, 1988 NUMBER 5
ACCOUNTANT MALPRACTICE

Issues Tested:

    I.   Fraud Under 10(b) and 10b-5
    II. Third Party Liability

Again, the student should know that the elements and defenses of negligence (e.g. lack of due care, assumption of the risk, etc.) have no place in a discussion of fraud. The student must also be prepared to discuss the "primary benefit" standard of *Ultramares*.

NOVEMBER, 1989 NUMBER 3
ACCOUNTANT LIABILITY

Issues Tested:

      I.   Constructive Fraud
     II.   Negligence

The candidate must be able to distinguish constructive fraud from negligence. Constructive fraud differs from actual/intentional fraud since constructive fraud does not require the defendant to have actual knowledge of the falsity (scienter). The defendant must either be grossly negligent or recklessly disregard the facts. Negligence is a reasonable standard. The candidate should distinguish the elements of constructive fraud and negligence.

MAY, 1990 NUMBER 5
ACCOUNTANT MALPRACTICE

Issues Tested:

      I.   Accountant-Client Privilege
     II.   Negligence
     III. 10b-5 Fraud
     IV. Third Party Liability

See above.

MAY, 1991 NUMBER 5
ACCOUNTANT MALPRACTICE

Issues Tested:

      I.   Fraud
     II.   Section 11 of the 1933 Securities Act
     III. 10(b) and 10b-5

Under Section 11 of the 1933 act, the plaintiff must prove that the accountant made material misstatement or omissions in the registration statement. The candidate should not think "fraud." The plaintiff only needs to show a loss on the transaction. There is no element of privity. The accountant can defend by showing due diligence.

MAY, 1992 NUMBER 3
ACCOUNTANT AS TRUSTEE

Issues Tested:

I. Standard of Care
II. Treatment of Beneficiaries
III. Fiduciary Duties

As discussed with the section on trusts, accountants as trustees must follow the "Prudent Trustee Rule." Therefore, the accountant can be sued in negligence for not using due care in the administration of the trust.

The accountant/trustee must treat the income and principal beneficiaries impartially. The trustee owes all beneficiaries fiduciary duties. These duties include the duties of care, skill, prudence, loyalty, accounting, and impartiality.

NOVEMBER, 1992 NUMBER 3
ACCOUNTANT LIABILITY

Issues Tested:

I. Negligence
II. Fraud
III. 10b-5 Fraud

See above.

MAY, 1995 NUMBER 4
CPA'S NEGLIGENCE AND FRAUD

Issues Tested:

I. Elements of Negligence
II. Elements of Fraud